Ruhlman's
HOW TO
SAUTÉ

ALSO BY MICHAEL RUHLMAN

RUHLMAN'S

HOW TO
SAUTÉ

foolproof techniques
and recipes for the
home cook

MICHAEL RUHLMAN

photographs by donna turner ruhlman

LITTLE, BROWN AND COMPANY
NEW YORK BOSTON LONDON

Little, Brown and Company
Hachette Book Group
1290 Avenue of the Americas, New York, NY 10104
littlebrown.com

First Edition: May 2016

Little, Brown and Company is a division of Hachette Book Group, Inc. The Little, Brown name and logo are trademarks of Hachette Book Group, Inc.

The publisher is not responsible for websites (or their content) that are not owned by the publisher.

The Hachette Speakers Bureau provides a wide range of authors for speaking events. To find out more, go to hachettespeakersbureau.com or call (866) 376-6591.

Library of Congress Cataloging-in-Publication Data

Ruhlman, Michael, date.
  Ruhlman's how to saute : foolproof techniques and recipes for the home cook / Michael Ruhlman ; photographs by Donna Turner Ruhlman. — First edition.
      pages cm.
  Includes index.
  ISBN 978-0-316-25415-1 (hc)
  1. Sauteing. I. Ruhlman, Donna Turner, photographer. II. Title.
  TX689.4.R84 2016
  641.7'7—dc23   2015027756
10 9 8 7 6 5 4 3 2 1
Design: Level, Calistoga, California
SC
Printed in China

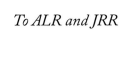

To ALR and JRR

CONTENTS

THE
HOT
SEAT

ONE OF THE GREAT FACTS OF COOKING IS THAT ONE
never stops learning how to do it: the knowledge of cooking runs as deep as
the ocean.

I began this book thinking that the sauté would be the simplest cooking technique to define, and yet I stumbled to articulate its precise meaning.
"Sauté" is among the most common words and techniques in the kitchen, but
it is far more elusive than we recognize. The aim of this book is to help you
master sauté's hidden complexities and nuances, which will make you an all-
around better cook—and to eat some delicious food as we learn.

When I teach a cooking technique, I think back to the place I first learned
it. This place is invariably my first cooking kitchen at the Culinary Institute
of America, where my chef instructor, Michael Pardus, announced with the
authority of an emperor: "'Sauté' means 'tender item cooked quickly over high
heat.'" He paused, looked at our class, and said, "You *cannot* sauté a lamb shank."

That made sense. If you were to sauté a lamb shank, you would end up
with something tough and inedible. A heavily worked muscle, streaked with
tendon and silverskin, sheathing a bone, takes hours in moist heat to become
tender—not just a few minutes in a pan on the stove.

In French, "sauté" means "to jump." When you push a pan forward and its
contents—English peas, for instance—run up the sloping sides and hop into

the air, you are jumping them. You are *sautéing* them. This is how we picture a chef sautéing—using the sloping sides of a pan to toss food into the air. Try *that* with a lamb shank!

Pardus also defined "sauté" as the most demanding station in a busy restaurant kitchen. We were learning to become professional cooks, and Pardus described the sauté station as the "hot seat" on the line, where the action is and where only the best cooks work.

At home, most cooks do not put out hundreds of plates of food in an evening, but the sauté remains the most common of the primary techniques we use to apply heat to food. (The others are roasting, braising, grilling, and poaching.) Indeed, the sauté is so common that we often overlook its countless nuances. But paying attention to the details makes everything we cook taste better.

I also learned about the sauté from another revered and accomplished chef at the Culinary Institute: its president, Ferdinand Metz. A lifelong cook, he began his career in America in the kitchen of Le Pavillon (a kitchen run by Pierre Franey and employing a young Jacques Pépin). At the time of our interview, he had been the CIA's president for more than fifteen years. He told me about the basic cooking methods, and about the process of learning which method to apply to which foods. The goal is to learn them so well that you don't need to think about them, which allows the cook's mind to be open.

"In sautéing," he said, German accent intact, "you could say, my God, there are probably ten different temperature levels.… Surely the principle is to encase the meat or fish by caramelizing the protein, but there are different levels that depend on what it is I'm doing. Some foods need a very harsh level; others need a very soft level that almost generates some moisture. It depends on what it is that you want to do. Whether it's chicken or bacon, all those things require different levels."

"Bacon?" I remember thinking. "You *sauté* bacon?" I always fried mine, but if Chef Metz said one sautéed bacon, then one sautéed bacon. Chicken and bacon represent two ends of the spectrum: chicken, a tender item, requires very high heat, while bacon, which is naturally tougher, requires gentle heat. And there my clean definition of "sauté"—high heat, tender item—began to blur.

As I prepared to write this book, I made lunch for one of my best friends—scrambled eggs and sautéed mushrooms, a toasted, buttered baguette, and a glass of white wine. Only then, as we talked about the book, did I realize what a tangled trick it was to define this most basic of cooking techniques. I tripped on my own words and eventually gave up and moved on to less complicated matters—the United States Congress, I believe.

And now, as I write, I return to that lunch in my mind. I called the mushrooms "sautéed." A reasonable and clear example: soft fungi cooked over very high heat in a little oil, then finished with some shallot, salt and pepper, a splash of white wine, and then, lowering the heat, a little butter, jumping the mushrooms in the pan to distribute and emulsify the butter in the wine and mushroom juices.

But what about the scrambled eggs—by that definition, aren't they, too, sautéed? I would never call them "sautéed eggs," yet I'd followed sauté principles and actions: food cooked in a low-sided pan in hot fat on the stovetop.

I changed tactics. "A sauté needs dry heat," I told my friend. She winced and shook her head, not understanding.

To be fair, I hadn't understood either when I first read it in my CIA textbook *The New Professional Chef.* Chapter nineteen: "Dry-Heat Cooking with Fats and Oils." How could it be *dry* heat if you're cooking in a fluid?

"Dry" turns out to have a specific meaning in this context, distinct as oil from water. According to my text, "dry" means that water is more or less absent. When water is involved, the temperature shifts down to first gear because water can't rise above 212°F/100°C. That temperature is too low to brown food, so with water present we can't develop the complex flavors that proteins, carbohydrates, and sugars take on at higher heat.

Dry heat allows for high heat, which generates browning and searing, colors we can see and know to be delicious. But, unlike poaching and braising, which happen in moist environments, the act of dry searing has no substantial tenderizing effect. Therefore, one can sauté over high heat only those foods that are already tender: a medallion of pork tenderloin, a chicken breast, a fillet of sole, asparagus, okra. Of course, items that are not naturally tender can be tenderized before cooking—by pounding veal scaloppine, for example.

But, then, what's the difference between sautéing and frying? Generally speaking, it is simply the amount of oil or other fat. Sautéing requires only a small amount of oil; in pan-frying, the oil comes halfway up the item being cooked; in deep-frying, the food is fully submerged.

My definition expanded once again: Sauté is a stovetop cooking technique wherein tender food is transformed in a shallow pan with a small amount of hot fat, usually over high heat. The heat does more than just warm the food—it creates flavor on the food's surface. In a short time that pork medallion or okra has been changed from raw and unappealing to visually enticing and delicious.

I came to realize that my response to my lunchtime companion should have begun thus:

To define "sauté," one must be flexible and open to variation and even contradiction.

Any form of shallow-pan cooking on the stovetop using dry heat (that is, a small amount of hot fat) can be considered a sauté, but 90 percent of the time "sauté" means exactly what Chef Pardus taught me: a tender object cooked quickly in fat.

Points of finesse are critical to the main techniques of applying heat to food. Understanding them is the key to becoming a great cook.

RUHLMAN'S

HOW TO
SAUTÉ

THE
BASICS

THE COOKING VESSEL

Your first important decision is choice of pan. A thin pan is harder to cook well in than a thick pan. There's only so much heat a thin pan can convey before a cool medallion of beef absorbs it. And if the pan is no longer hot, the meat will stick.

A stainless-steel sauté pan with a thick, heavy bottom is ideal.

In culinary school we were taught that a proper sauté pan, called a *sauteuse*, has sloping sides, which allows you to jump the food in the pan. A pan with straight sides, on the other hand, is referred to as a *sautoire*.

One must, of course, address the nonstick pan, perhaps the single most harmful addition to the modern kitchen in terms of preventing us from becoming better cooks. If you heat your pan properly and allow the oil to become hot before you add the meat, and if you resist the temptation to move the meat the moment it hits the pan because you're afraid it is going to stick (which it will; the trick is to let it release on its own), you will not have an issue with food sticking. Indeed, that your meat does not stick to your pristine stainless-steel pan with hot fat in it is an indication that you are cooking it properly.

Nonstick pans are not bad in and of themselves; I own two very good nonstick pans (12 inches/30 centimeters and 8 inches/20 centimeters) and am grateful for them. I cook eggs in them because the protein in eggs is eager to stick to a steel surface unless the cooking oil is super hot, which you don't want for scrambled eggs or an omelet. When I cook a fish that is too delicate to withstand the high heat required to keep it from sticking to steel, I use a nonstick pan. And anything very starchy, such as potatoes or spaetzle, will stick to steel; to get good browning on a starch without its sticking, I use a nonstick pan.

The size of the sauté pan is critical. A too-big pan requires you to use more fat and perhaps to deliver more heat than you may want or need; a too-small pan forces you to crowd your food. Choose a pan that will allow you to spread individual items out comfortably—as a rule, leave a half inch or so between them. Crowding your food in the pan cools the pan to the point that your food steams rather than sears, losing flavor and never achieving that appealing color. It also increases the chance your food will stick to the pan, and makes getting your food to the right temperature more difficult.

This deserves repeating:

Don't crowd your pan!
It's always better to choose a pan
that's too big than too small.

If you have too much food for even your biggest pan, sauté in batches, leaving the first batch slightly underdone so that it can finish cooking in the gentle ambient heat of a low oven (200°F/95°C) while you work on the next batch.

THE FAT

The next decision: which fat to choose? Oil is a fat, but not all fats are oils. Reach first for economical vegetable oils like safflower, soybean, peanut, corn, or canola. They're good cooking fats because they're neutral in flavor and have a high smoke point—about 450°F/230°C—which means they get very hot before they start smoking. (Once oil begins smoking, it degrades quickly, so you need to get the food in the pan immediately or get the pan off the heat. Not only is the oil's flavor changing, but it is releasing a flammable vapor that will eventually ignite. If this happens, don't freak out—just put a lid or baking sheet on the pan. Whatever you do, *never* throw water on burning oil.)

A superlative vegetable oil for sautéing is grapeseed oil, but it's a little costly for everyday use.

Olive oil has a relatively low smoke point; too much heat degrades the flavorful oil and can give the food an off or bitter flavor. Many chefs routinely sauté in olive oil, but I discourage it: if it's good olive oil, you'll ruin it with high heat, and if it's not good olive oil, why are you even using it? It's better to use neutral vegetable oils for high-heat sautés, and save your tasty olive oils to flavor the food after it's cooked. I do occasionally use an all-purpose generic olive oil (not extra-virgin) for quickly cooked vegetables for its flavor.

Coconut oil is now readily available and is great to cook with. It has an almost sweet, tropical flavor, which I like for Asian-inspired sautés.

Rendered animal fat is an excellent cooking medium, whether from beef, chicken, or pork. Beef and chicken are especially flavorful fats; pork fat is notable for its mild flavor and also its abundance. These animal fats have a lower smoke point than vegetable oils; they begin to break down and take on bad flavors at 375°F/190°C.

A fat of special note is clarified butter. Whole butter is composed of milk fat, milk proteins, and water. When you sauté in whole butter, the pan will be relatively cool until the water cooks off, at which point the milk proteins will brown and eventually burn. But when you clarify the butter first, which involves removing the water and milk solids, you end up with an especially flavorful cooking fat that can get as hot as any animal fat without burning.

The traditional method of clarifying butter is to melt it in a pan over low heat, then skim off the solids that eventually coagulate and rise to the surface as the water cooks out of it. The clear fat is then ladled into a container and can be refrigerated for up to 10 days or frozen for a few months. (It tends to absorb other flavors if stored for longer than that.) A quicker way to make clarified butter at home is to melt it in a measuring glass in a microwave. Most of the water, whey, and solids will sink to the bottom; you can easily skim off any solids that float to the top. Then you are left with just the clear fat on top.

THE HEAT

Cooks sauté at a range of temperatures. The right level of heat depends on the qualities of what you are cooking and what your final goal is—low heat to render the fat in a strip of bacon, high heat for a meat medallion or vegetables that you want to brown for flavor. When we sauté proteins such as meat or fish, we most often want to create good flavor by searing them. Searing is often called caramelizing (which technically refers to the browning of sugar) because of the brown color associated with it, but it is more precisely a result of the Maillard reaction.

The Maillard reaction gives us countless complex and nuanced flavors responsible for a food's deliciousness.

Imagine the flavor of boiled broccoli or cauliflower, then compare it in your mind to the flavor of the same vegetable that's been deeply browned through frying or roasting. The Maillard reaction is responsible for the enormous differences in taste and complexity.

A good sear on meat—the kind of hot, quick cooking that results in a crisp, brown crust—is also a Maillard reaction. Searing does not "seal in" juices, but it does enhance meat's flavor and texture. A good sear gives us complex flavors and a crisp counterpoint to the soft interior of the meat. You almost always want good color when you are sautéing meat, because that color means flavor.

In order to get that good color, we need high, dry heat. While the Maillard reaction can begin at 250°F/120°C (with bread, for instance), we wouldn't want to cook a piece of meat at that temperature: by the time the surface browned, if it browned at all, the interior would be overcooked. With tender, juicy cuts of meat, we want to make that browning happen as quickly as possible, to get that flavor jolt before bringing the food to the right internal temperature.

But what if you don't want browning? Then you don't want to sauté over high heat. For instance, to preserve the freshness of the fava beans and corn in my succotash (page 41), I sauté over moderate heat.

We use low heat for effects that require time, such as rendering and tenderizing. For bacon we want to both render the fat and tenderize the meat, so it's best to sauté bacon over low heat. For duck breast (page 69), we have to render the fat before we can achieve a crisp skin, one of the great pleasures of duck, so the duck is cooked skin-down over the lowest possible heat to render the fat without overcooking the meat.

SALTING

Salting what you're cooking is of the utmost importance, no matter what technique you use to cook it.

But *when* you salt is just as critical as *how much* you salt.

Salt meat long enough before cooking so that the salt dissolves and has time to penetrate the meat. The earlier you salt, the better, but even 20 minutes for a chicken breast makes a big difference in flavor. If you salt meat just before putting it in the pan, half of the salt will fall off as you cook it, and you will have an underseasoned piece of meat.

Fish is so delicate that the large grains of kosher salt can actually "burn" the flesh—that is, denature the protein—and the seasoning will be uneven. Fish should therefore be salted lightly with fine sea salt just before sautéing, and then finished with a very light salting after it's cooked, if you wish.

Vegetables should be salted after they're in the pan and cooking. The same goes for fruits if you're using them in a savory preparation. Salt draws abundant water—the enemy of the sauté technique—from fruits and vegetables.

TEMPERING

Tempering meat and fish is important for any cut that is more than ½ inch/12 millimeters thick.

Tempering simply means removing the meat or fish from the refrigerator so that it has time to come to room temperature—

30 to 60 minutes for fish and 4 hours or so for meat, depending on the thickness of the cut and the warmth of the kitchen. The goal of the sauté is to achieve a flavorful browned crust and a uniform interior temperature; putting a piece of cold meat in a hot pan can result in an overcooked exterior with a cold center. Tempering will help you cook meat perfectly.

RESTING

After cooking meat in any form of dry-heat cooking (grilling, broiling, roasting, sautéing), resting the meat is critical. Letting the meat sit off the heat facilitates the redistribution of the juices throughout the cut and allows the heat concentrated at the exterior of the meat to even out throughout the meat. In fact, when you remove the meat from the pan, it should be slightly under-cooked—"carryover cooking" will finish the meat. Meat stays hot for a long time, so don't be tempted to cover it with foil or it will overcook. (Resting is not necessary for fish or vegetables.)

FLOURING OR DRYING

Because nothing cools down a pan (and ruins a sear) like water, any moisture that is on meat or fish will precipitously drop the temperature of your pan and the oil in it. That change in temperature can result in food sticking to the pan, and can generate so much steam that the food doesn't brown well. Both of these unfortunate scenarios can be avoided either by lightly flouring the meat or by blotting it dry with a paper towel.

If you've salted meat ahead and it has a very moist surface, be sure to blot it dry before sautéing it.

Flouring meat or fish creates a moisture-free surface and gives you an additional element to brown for more flavor and texture. Sometimes the flour or the browned bits sticking to the pan will burn. If this happens, clean your pan before sautéing the next batch or making a pan sauce.

JUMPING

As noted, when we think of sautéing, we imagine a chef flipping or tossing food into the air and catching it all masterfully in the pan. There is no special trick other than common sense and practice. As Chef Pardus instructed us, "Practice it here so you don't piss off your mom at home when you spill the food all over the stovetop." He also suggested practicing with dried beans (and no heat), which is a clever idea.

The reasons for jumping food in the pan are convenience and efficiency. Jumping the food quickly flips it and distributes it in the pan, so the food cooks evenly without requiring you to use a utensil.

BREADING AND PAN-FRYING

One of the ways you can sauté meat is with a technique called a pan-fry, which is a shallow-pan, dry-heat technique that uses a little more fat than a traditional sauté. You'll find this technique used for two preparations in the book, the chicken schnitzel (page 53) and the chicken-fried steak (page 113). We pan-fry thick items for which we want an evenly cooked crust. You don't always have to bread or coat the item, but it invariably tastes better when you do. The abundant oil also helps cook the meat more evenly and quickly.

There are two options for breading: simply dredging the meat or fish in bread crumbs or, for a thicker and fuller encasement of the meat, using what's known in culinary schools as "standard breading procedure." In this method, the meat or fish is first floured to create a dry surface, then coated in egg wash, and finally dredged in bread crumbs.

My bread crumbs of choice are panko. These Japanese bread crumbs are large, coarse, and dry, so they resist absorbing oil and remain especially crunchy. Because the main goal of breading and pan-frying is to create a crisp crust, it's only logical that you should choose a coating that guarantees crispness.

SAUCES

A sauté done properly does not create its own sauce, but we often rely on sauces to finish a dish. This book concludes with a variety of sauces, each representing a different technique. You'll find that these sauces pair excellently with sautéed foods—from the very simple, such as a traditional pan sauce made in the same sauté pan the meat cooked in (page 148), to something more refined, such as a classic béchamel (page 160). I've also included recipes for things that we don't typically consider "sauce," such as guacamole (page 158), which is fabulous on pork, chicken, and lean fish.

THE
RECIPES

THE ICON:
VEAL SCALOP-PINE

THERE IS NO MORE EMBLEMATIC SAUTÉ THAN VEAL SCALOPPINE—
thinly sliced top round of veal, quickly sautéed and served with a simple pan
sauce. It hews to all the tenets of dry-heat, shallow-pan cooking: It's tender,
having been pounded thin. It's dusted with flour to ensure that the surface
is dry and so won't stick to the pan; the flour also contributes to the flavorful,
browned crust, and residual flour in the pan will help thicken the pan sauce. It
was the opening dish on the sauté station in my Introduction to Hot Foods class
in culinary school for a reason. It truly is the iconic example of a good sauté.

I also love this dish for its simplicity and for the way a citrusy or vinous sauce
accentuates the veal's mild flavor. Use the best-quality veal you can find. Well-
raised veal will have a dark pink color and rich flavor; look for farm-raised veal
at Whole Foods Market or a local butcher offering source-verified meat.

Marcella Hazan, the late cookbook author and cooking teacher, writes in
her *Essentials of Classic Italian Cooking* that for the best scaloppine, one should
procure a good top round (from the inner back leg of the animal), slice it
thinly across the grain, and pound it until it's very thin. I find that using a
meat mallet with some kind of teeth is best, as this cut needs to be tenderized
mechanically (that is, by pounding it physically, rather than just by cooking it).
Failing to pound it thin enough will result in a tougher finished dish.

This preparation is incredibly versatile. Hazan offers about a dozen variations—scaloppine with capers, with anchovies, with ham, with mozzarella—and she also wraps the scaloppine around other ingredients to make stuffed veal dishes. I'm offering this ultra-simple version, then another later on that features sautéed mushrooms and Marsala wine (page 75). Here, I make a basic pan sauce using wine, a technique I explore further on pages 148 to 151. This dish goes beautifully with pasta with garlic and olive oil and a salad.

4 (5-ounce/150-gram) slices veal top round

Kosher salt

Freshly ground black pepper

Flour

2 tablespoons vegetable oil

1 to 2 tablespoons minced shallot

¼ cup/60 milliliters dry white wine

2 tablespoons fresh lemon juice

3 tablespoons/45 grams butter

1 tablespoon chopped fresh parsley

SERVES 4

- If you'll be cooking the veal in batches, **PREHEAT** the oven to 200°F/95°C.

- **PLACE** each veal slice between two sheets of plastic wrap and **POUND** with a meat mallet or skillet to a thickness of about ¼ inch/5 millimeters. **SEASON** the scaloppine with salt and pepper.

- **PUT** enough flour for coating the veal on a plate—½ cup/70 grams or so.

- **SET** a large sauté pan over high heat. **DREDGE** the veal in the flour and **SHAKE** off the excess. When the pan is hot, **ADD** the vegetable oil. **SWIRL** it around the pan until it's hot. **LOWER** the heat to medium-high and **LAY** two or four of the floured scaloppine in the hot oil, depending on the size of your pan—they should not be touching each other. **COOK** the veal till you've developed a nice browned crust, about 60 seconds. **FLIP** the veal and **REPEAT** on the other side. If you're cooking the veal in batches, **HOLD** the cooked veal in the warm oven while you **SAUTE** the rest.

- When all the veal is done, **ADD** the shallot to the empty pan and **SAUTE** till heated through, 15 or 20 seconds. **ADD** the wine and **COOK**, scraping up any flour stuck to the pan, until the wine has reduced by two-thirds, then **ADD** the lemon juice. When the liquid returns to a simmer, **SWIRL** in the butter and **CONTINUE** to swirl or stir until all the butter is melted. Then **ADD** the parsley and **STIR** or **SWIRL** the sauce to distribute the herb.

- **RETURN** the veal to the pan to rewarm and coat each side with the sauce. **SERVE** immediately, spooning any remaining sauce over the veal.

Step 1. Sauté the floured veal until it's nicely browned on both sides.

Step 2. After the veal is cooked, add the shallots and sauté until softened, then deglaze the pan with wine.

Step 3. The wine will simmer and reduce, loosening the browned bits in the pan.

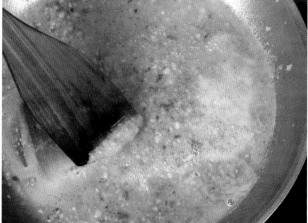

Step 4. Dredge a flat-edged spatula across the pan to lift the browned bits into the wine.

Step 5. When the wine has reduced, add the butter.

Step 6. Swirl the pan continuously until all the butter is emulsified into the sauce.

Step 7. Season the sauce with freshly chopped parsley.

Step 8. Return the veal to the pan to reheat and to coat it with the sauce.

SAUTÉED MUSH-ROOMS (AND HOW TO TURN THEM INTO A SAUCE OR A SOUP)

I MAKE THESE AS OFTEN AS POSSIBLE BECAUSE THEY'RE SO simple, economical, and delicious. Their earthy but subtle flavor and umami effect make mushrooms a suitable accompaniment to most meats and fish and a perfect flavoring device for any starch—pasta, rice, or heartier grains such as barley or wheat berries.

Fresh wild mushrooms offer the greatest variety of flavors and textures, but even the ubiquitous white button mushroom can be brought to flavorful heights if you apply a little oomph. The key is a super hot sauté to brown the mushrooms. You're working against the clock, because mushrooms want to release their copious water, so you need to brown them over high heat as fast as possible. Once there's liquid in the pan, no more browning can happen. At that point, we turn the heat to low, season aggressively with salt and pepper, and then continue to cook the mushrooms in wine and butter.

When you know how to sauté mushrooms for maximum flavor, you have numerous dishes at your fingertips. By themselves they are delicious, but you can also manipulate their texture to turn them into a fabulous pureed sauce or cream of mushroom soup. This technique of sautéing and then pureeing works with more vegetables than not; try the ones listed on page 24.

2 tablespoons vegetable or grapeseed oil

1 pound/450 grams white button mushrooms, brushed clean or quickly rinsed and dried, cut in ½-inch/12-millimeter slices

Kosher salt

1 tablespoon minced shallot

Freshly ground black pepper

Curry powder (optional)

¼ cup/60 milliliters dry white wine

2 to 3 tablespoons cold butter (the more, the better in my opinion), cut into a few pieces

SERVES 2 TO 4

- **HAVE** all your ingredients ready and next to the stovetop. Also **HAVE** ready a large offset stainless-steel spatula or some other tool for pressing down on the mushrooms as soon as they go into the pan.

- **HEAT** a large, heavy-duty sauté pan over high heat for a few minutes, until it is very hot. When the pan is hot, **ADD** the oil. **SWIRL** the oil in the pan so it coats the entire surface. **ADD** the mushrooms in one layer and **PRESS** down hard on them to get as much surface-area browning as possible. When they are browned on one side, about 2 minutes, **FLIP** or **JUMP** them to brown the other side, pressing down hard as before.

- **ADD** a four-finger pinch of salt, followed by the shallot. **CONTINUE** to flip or turn the mushrooms so that they cook through, another 30 seconds or so, adding many grinds of pepper as they cook. **TOSS** in a pinch of curry powder, too, if you wish.

- **ADD** the wine to deglaze the pan. When three-quarters of the wine has cooked off, **ADD** the butter, swirling the pan continuously until all the butter has melted, and then **TURN** the heat to low until you're ready to serve.

- **SERVE** the mushrooms hot, or **ALLOW** them to cool to room temperature and gently **WARM** them when you need them. They can be done several hours in advance before reheating to serve.

Mushroom Sauce

This all-purpose mushroom sauce is made by adding a little liquid to sautéed mushrooms and pureeing them. Simple. The sauce should be a thick puree; for a more refined sauce, pass it through a fine-mesh strainer before serving. Or serve the sauce without pureeing it at all, as I do for Veal Marsala (page 75).

**1 recipe Sautéed Mushrooms
(page 19; you can omit the butter or include it,
depending on how rich you want your sauce to be)**

**½ cup/120 milliliters cream or half-and-half
(or water or mushroom stock)**

Kosher salt

Freshly ground black pepper

Squeeze of lemon (optional)

MAKES ABOUT 1½ CUPS/360 MILLILITERS

- When the mushrooms have finished sautéing, **TURN** the heat to medium and **ADD** the cream or half-and-half. **BRING** to a gentle simmer, then **TURN** the heat to low and **ALLOW** the liquid to become infused, a minute or two.

- **TRANSFER** the mushrooms and liquid to a blender and **PUREE** (remember to **REMOVE** the center piece of the lid and **COVER** the hole with a towel, or the hot puree may burst out of the blender). **TASTE** and **ADJUST** for seasoning, adding more salt and pepper if needed, followed by a squeeze of lemon (½ teaspoon or so) if you wish. **SERVE** as is or strained through a fine-mesh strainer.

Easy Cream of Mushroom Soup

To make cream of mushroom soup, simply increase the amount of liquid you add to the mushroom sauce. Half-and-half will produce a rich, hearty soup. For an enormously decadent and delicious soup, use cream (but you would want to offer servings of at most ½ cup/120 milliliters). To make a nondairy soup, you can use water, but it will of course be a little thinner; if you have the time and inclination, you can simmer the mushroom stems in the water first, then strain them out.

For a superlative starter course, I recommend sautéing an additional half batch of mushrooms, chopping the half batch, and adding them to the soup for more flavor, visual appeal, and texture. Minced fresh chives or parsley makes an excellent finishing touch for this soup.

1½ recipes Sautéed Mushrooms (page 19)

**1 cup/240 milliliters cream or half-and-half
(or more as desired)**

Kosher salt

Freshly ground black pepper

Squeeze of lemon (optional)

**1 tablespoon minced fresh chives or parsley,
for garnish (optional)**

SERVES 4 (FIRST-COURSE PORTIONS)

- When the mushrooms have finished sautéing, **REMOVE** a third of them from the pan to a cutting board. **TURN** the heat to medium and **ADD** the cream or half-and-half. **BRING** to a gentle simmer, then **TURN** the heat to low and **ALLOW** the liquid to become infused.

- **TRANSFER** the mushrooms to a blender and **PUREE** (remember to **REMOVE** the center piece of the blender lid and **COVER** with a towel or the hot puree may burst out of the blender). **TASTE** and **ADJUST** for seasoning, adding more salt and pepper if needed, followed by a squeeze of lemon (½ teaspoon or so) if you wish. **CHOP** the reserved mushrooms and **STIR** into the soup. **GARNISH** with fresh herbs, if using, and **SERVE**.

Like mushrooms, any of the following vegetables can be sautéed, simmered in half-and-half, and pureed to make soup or sauce. Brown them for more caramelized flavor, or sauté them over lower heat for a purer vegetable flavor.

- Asparagus
- Beets
- Carrots
- Corn
- Red bell peppers
- Snap peas
- Spinach
- Tomatoes
- Turnips

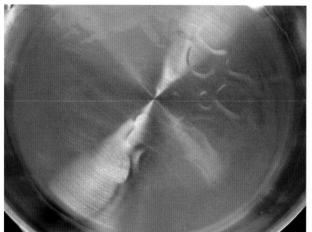

Step 1. The key to great seared mushrooms is to get the pan very hot before adding oil; the oil should ripple and pool when you add it.

Step 2. When the oil is smoking hot, add the mushrooms in one layer.

Step 3. Press the mushrooms down hard against the pan to facilitate browning.

Step 4. Season them with salt and plenty of freshly ground black pepper.

Step 5. Add the shallot and sauté until tender.

Step 6. Add the wine and cook it down till the pan is almost dry.

Step 7. Add the cream or half-and-half.

Step 8. Cook the sauce down by about half, then serve or keep warm till ready to serve.

SAUTÉED SPINACH WITH GARLIC

THIS IS ONE OF THE EASIEST AND FASTEST SAUTÉS, AND THUS a frequent side dish in my repertoire. It's also densely nutritious, and goes with just about any meat or fish. Put a poached egg on top and it becomes a main course. Just make sure you start with enough spinach, as it seriously cooks down: 4 loose cups of raw spinach will cook down to less than 1 cup when finished. You may want to cook it in batches; it can also be cooked ahead and gently rewarmed in a little butter.

Sauté the spinach in olive oil or, for more flavor, butter. You can cook it to whatever point you wish—sometimes I want it all cooked down, other times I like to keep some of the spinach warm but raw, so that it doesn't collapse. To enhance it, you can add 8 ounces/225 grams of mushrooms, sautéed (see page 19), or ½ cup/120 milliliters cream.

2 teaspoons olive oil or butter

2 to 4 garlic cloves, minced

1½ pounds/675 grams spinach

Kosher salt

Freshly ground black pepper

SERVES 4

- **HEAT** the oil or butter in a large sauté pan over medium-high heat and **ADD** the garlic. **SAUTE** the garlic until it's tender. **ADD** the spinach, turning the heat to low if you prefer your spinach less cooked. **USE** tongs to turn the spinach when the bottom layer has cooked and collapsed and to distribute the garlic. **ADD** salt and pepper to taste as it cooks. **REMOVE** the pan from the heat when the spinach is almost to the doneness you want, as it will continue to cook down off the heat. **SERVE** at once, or **SET** aside to be reheated when the rest of your dishes are ready.

Step 1. Sauté the garlic in oil till it's almost cooked through.

Step 2. Add the spinach.

Step 3. Use tongs to turn the spinach, flipping top to bottom as the bottom layers wilt.

Step 4. You can remove the spinach now, when some of the leaves have yet to wilt, or continue cooking till they are all thoroughly wilted (as on page 28).

SAUTÉED ASPARA-GUS

ASPARAGUS SPEARS ARE LOVELY COOKED IN JUST ABOUT any fashion. I like to sauté them because they develop a more complex flavor than when boiled or steamed. Because intense heat is not required to cook them through, I use olive oil. I flavor the oil and the asparagus with minced garlic and finish the asparagus with lemon zest. The tips cook more quickly than the stems, so I peel asparagus unless they are very thin and tender. I take pleasure in the peeling, transforming the woody stalk into an elegant and beautiful vegetable to cook and serve.

Olive oil

1 or 2 garlic cloves, minced

1 pound/450 grams asparagus, ends removed and stalks peeled

Kosher salt

Freshly grated lemon zest (use a Microplane if you have one)

SERVES 4

- **SET** a sauté pan, large enough to accommodate the asparagus in one layer, over medium heat. **POUR** in just enough olive oil to coat the bottom of the pan. **ADD** the garlic and **STIR** to coat it with the olive oil. When it has cooked long enough to become tender but not brown, 20 to 30 seconds, **ADD** the asparagus and **COOK** till heated through, a few minutes, rolling them in the pan to cook them evenly. **SEASON** with salt as you cook. **REMOVE** the asparagus to a platter and scatter the lemon zest over the top. **SERVE**.

Step 1. If your asparagus has tough stems, peel them; this also makes for an elegant appearance.

Step 2. When the garlic is tender but not browned, add the asparagus and sauté.

Step 3. Season with salt.

Step 4. The asparagus can be kept warm in the pan while you finish the rest of the meal.

SAUTÉED CARROTS AND CELERY

THE MYSTERIES OF MIREPOIX—ONION, CARROT, AND CELERY, the beginnings of so many dishes—continue to astonish me. Somehow it seems to make everything better, from braises to sauces to soups. I'd been making a spicy beef stir-fry (page 127) for years before it dawned on me that part of the magic of that dish was the pairing of the carrots and celery with the beef.

This quick and economical sauté is a great accompaniment to any kind of beef or even venison. You can throw in some chopped shallot or onion for more depth and sweetness, returning to the exquisite effects of traditional mirepoix; I prefer to leave the onion out to concentrate the beef-carrot flavor. I've added caraway here, but you can use any seasoning that would pair well with whatever main course you're serving—garlic, cumin, parsley, chives, or even cayenne.

Use a mandoline to make the julienne uniform.

2 teaspoons caraway seeds (optional)

2 teaspoons vegetable oil

2 large carrots, julienned

2 large celery ribs, julienned

Kosher salt

Freshly ground black pepper

SERVES 4

- If using caraway seeds (or any whole spices), **PUT** them in a large sauté pan over high heat. When the pan is hot, **ADD** the oil. When the oil is hot, **ADD** the carrots and celery and **TOSS** or **SAUTE** until tender, 60 to 90 seconds, adding salt and pepper to taste. **REMOVE** them from the heat; they'll keep while you finish the other courses.

FAVA BEAN
SUCCOTASH

THIS IS ONE OF MY FAVORITE VEGETABLE PREPARATIONS, thanks to its deep, rich flavors and colors. It's also an ideal way to show what a sauté really looks like, because the best way to mix and cook all the ingredients is to jump them in the pan. Succotash is especially good in midsummer, when both fresh favas and corn are widely available. If you can find fresh soybeans (edamame), they can replace the favas.

The bacon is sautéed gently to render the fat, and the onion is sautéed in that fat till tender; then the heat is increased, the favas and corn are sautéed, and it's finished with a little half-and-half and butter.

1 pound/450 grams fresh fava beans, shelled

2 thick bacon slices, cut into thin strips

½ onion, cut into small dice

Kosher salt

Corn kernels cut from 2 ears

½ cup/120 milliliters half-and-half

Freshly ground black pepper

2 tablespoons/30 grams butter

SERVES 4

- **BRING** a large pot of salted water to a vigorous boil over high heat and **ADD** the beans. **PREPARE** an ice bath. **COOK** the beans till they are tender, 2 to 3 minutes. **REMOVE** the beans to the ice bath. **STIR** them around so that they cool rapidly. **PEEL** off the dull green skins and **SET** the vibrantly green beans aside.

- In a large sauté pan, **SAUTE** the bacon over medium-low heat until it's tender and the fat has begun to render. Just as the bacon is beginning to brown, **ADD** the onion and a four-finger pinch of salt. **TURN** the heat to medium and **COOK** the onion till it's tender. **INCREASE** the heat to medium-high and **ADD** the corn and fava beans; sauté for a minute or so just to heat them through. **ADD** the half-and-half and several grinds of pepper, followed by the butter. **COOK**, stirring or jumping the succotash in the pan, until the liquid has reduced by half, another minute or so, or until it looks deliciously sauced. **SERVE** immediately.

SAUTÉED CHICKEN BREASTS
WITH WINE AND HERB PAN SAUCE

SAUTÉED CHICKEN BREASTS MIGHT BE THE MOST COMMON weeknight meal in America. But despite those who denounce this convenient cut of meat, it is delicious when prepared properly, especially with a quick wine and butter sauce made in the pan. Chefs denigrate the boneless, *skinless* chicken breast in particular, not so much because it is one of the most taste-free cuts of meat available, but because of what it symbolizes: Americans' slavish embrace of bland, low-fat food. Here, browned skin and a good pan sauce elevate the otherwise ordinary cut. The recipe hews to the fundamental tenets of the sauté: a tender cut of meat cooked quickly in a small amount of oil over high heat.

While the chicken breasts rest, complete the dish with a simple pan sauce: deglaze the pan with wine and shallot, mount it with butter, and finish it with fresh herbs. (For further notes on making pan sauces, see page 148.)

One of the most critical parts of this preparation is the pounding of the thicker part of the breast so that the piece has a fairly uniform thickness. The chicken is then seasoned with salt. While the pan heats, blot the chicken's skin so that it hits the oil dry. Once they're in the pan, don't move the pieces of chicken until they've cooked for at least 2 minutes. The skin will stick at first but will pull away from the pan as it cooks.

4 boneless, skin-on chicken breasts

Kosher salt

Vegetable oil

1 tablespoon minced shallot

½ cup/120 milliliters dry white wine

¼ cup/60 grams butter, cut into pieces

**2 tablespoons minced fresh parsley
(or any combination of parsley, chives, and tarragon)**

SERVES 4

- **PLACE** one chicken breast between two sheets of plastic wrap and **FLATTEN** the thicker end by pounding it with a meat mallet or a skillet, till the chicken is more or less of uniform thickness. **REPEAT** with the other pieces. **SEASON** each piece with salt.

- **SET** a large sauté pan over high heat for a couple of minutes, then **POUR** in enough oil so that a thin film coats the bottom. **BLOT** the chicken's skin dry with a paper towel. When the oil is rippling and just about to smoke, **LAY** the breasts in the pan, skin-side down, and **COOK** without moving them until the skin is browned and no longer sticks to the pan, 2 to 3 minutes. **REDUCE** the heat to medium-high, **FLIP** the breasts, and **COOK** for another few minutes, until they are just cooked through (they should be firm to the touch). Remember, they will continue to cook while you make the sauce.

- **REMOVE** the chicken to a plate. **POUR** off any oil remaining in the pan and **RETURN** it to the burner over medium-high heat. **ADD** the shallot and **STIR** briefly to soften it. **ADD** the wine and **SCRAPE** up any browned bits stuck to the pan. When half of the wine has cooked off, **ADD** the butter and **SWIRL** the pan continuously until all the butter has melted. **TURN** the flame to low, **ADD** the parsley, and **SWIRL** the pan to distribute it throughout the sauce. **RETURN** the chicken to the pan to rewarm. **SERVE**, topping the breasts with the sauce.

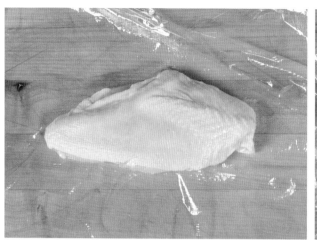

Step 1. Place each chicken breast between sheets of plastic wrap.

Step 2. Pound the breasts to a uniform thickness.

Step 3. Pounding helps to tenderize the chicken as well as give it uniform thickness for even cooking.

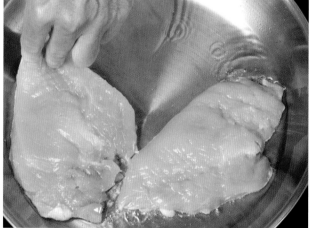

Step 4. When the oil in the pan is rippling hot, lay the breasts skin-side down. Resist the urge to move them.

Step 5. When the skin properly browns, the breasts will pull away from the pan.

Step 6. Cook the other side till they are almost but not quite done, then remove them from the pan.

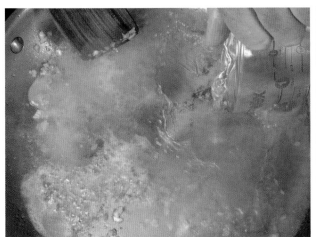

Step 7. Add the shallot and sauté till tender, then deglaze the pan with wine.

Step 8. Scrape the bottom of the pan as the wine reduces to lift up any browned bits.

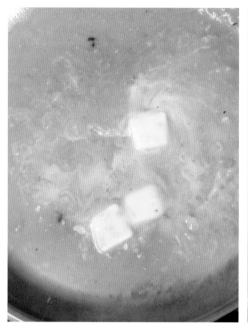

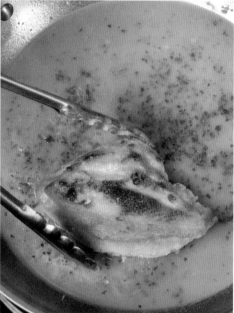

Step 9. When the wine has reduced by half, add the butter and swirl until it's emulsified into the sauce.

Step 10. Add the parsley and return the chicken to the pan to reheat and finish cooking.

Step 11. Spoon hot sauce over the chicken as it reheats.

Step 12. Serve, spooning the pan sauce over each breast.

CHICKEN SCHNIT-ZEL
WITH SAGE SPAETZLE

SCHNITZEL IS TRADITIONALLY ASSOCIATED WITH VIENNESE cuisine, but various forms of breaded, fried pieces of meat are found all over the world. Pan-frying uses a little more oil than a customary sauté, but the standard breading formula—flour (with lots of pepper), egg wash, and panko—can be used for just about any cut you might sauté.

Boneless chicken thighs make superior schnitzel because the meat is flavorful and can withstand intense heat. Schnitzel keeps remarkably well, so you can sauté it and keep it in a 300°F/150°C oven for up to a half hour before serving, allowing you to finish preparing the meal. I like to serve schnitzel with spaetzle, although pasta or roasted or mashed potatoes would go nicely, too. The spaetzle can be cooked and shocked in ice water ahead of time and reheated as needed.

This schnitzel is economical and delicious, and I like to top it with a tart sauce such as a classic rémoulade with capers, cornichons, and fresh herbs (page 152). It's also delicious with a simple squeeze of lemon.

4 boneless, skinless chicken thighs

Kosher salt

Freshly ground black pepper

1½ cups/200 grams flour

2 eggs, blended to uniformity

1½ cups/100 grams panko

Vegetable oil

SERVES 4

- **SEASON** the chicken with salt and pepper and **LET** rest for at least 10 minutes. **COMBINE** the flour with 2 tablespoons pepper and **MIX** to disperse the pepper. **DREDGE** the chicken in the flour, **DIP** it in the egg, then **COAT** it in the panko.

- **SET** a large sauté pan or *sautoire* over high heat. **POUR** in a ¼-inch/5-millimeter layer of oil; it should come well up the sides of the chicken when all the pieces are in the pan. When the oil is rippling and hot, **LAY** the chicken in, **REDUCE** the heat to medium-high, and **COOK** until golden brown on one side, 3 minutes or so. **FLIP** and **COOK** the other side as well. **CONTINUE** to flip and cook to get uniform browning and ensure that they are piping hot all the way through. Thighs are difficult to overcook—because of the fat, they will remain juicy.

- **REMOVE** to a rack or paper towel–lined plate. **SERVE** immediately or **KEEP** warm in a low oven until ready to serve.

Step 1. Standard breading procedure, right to left: meat is floured, then dipped in egg wash, then dredged in panko bread crumbs.

Step 2. It's best to keep the breaded chicken on a rack so that the underside stays dry.

Step 3. Sauté the chicken in enough oil so that its uneven surface comes completely into contact with the oil.

Step 4. Cook until both sides are nicely browned.

Sage Spaetzle

Spaetzle, literally "little sparrow" in German, is one of my favorite pastas. As it's associated with Eastern European cuisine, it's a perfect bed for chicken schnitzel. This version is flavored with a classic combination of sage and brown butter. The spaetzle is cooked and chilled in advance—up to 3 days in the refrigerator or a month in the freezer—then sautéed to finish.

2 eggs

⅔ cup/160 milliliters milk

1 cup/150 grams flour

¼ cup/8 grams minced fresh sage

1 teaspoon kosher salt

Freshly ground black pepper

1 tablespoon olive oil

2 tablespoons/30 grams butter

SERVES 4

- **COMBINE** the eggs, milk, flour, sage, salt, and several grindings of pepper in a bowl, **STIR** to mix well, then **COVER** and **LET** sit at room temperature for 30 minutes or **REFRIGERATE** for up to 24 hours.

- **BRING** a large pot of water to a boil with enough salt so that it tastes seasoned. **POUR** the batter into a spaetzle maker, a large perforated spoon, or a colander with large holes, and **PRESS** the batter through the holes so that it drips in strands into the boiling water. **COOK** the spaetzle until it floats, then **STRAIN** and **RINSE** under cold water until chilled. **DRAIN** well and **TOSS** with the olive oil. **COVER** until you're ready to serve— **REFRIGERATE** or **FREEZE** the spaetzle if you won't be finishing it within the next few hours.

- To serve, **MELT** the butter in a large sauté pan over high heat. After the frothing has subsided and the butter begins to turn brown, **ADD** the spaetzle and **SAUTE**, stirring and jumping them occasionally but allowing them to brown on the bottom of the pan. When lightly browned and hot, **SERVE**.

Step 1. I use a rubber spatula to press the batter through a deep perforated spoon, but a traditional spaetzle cutter works as well.

Step 2. Finish the cooled spaetzle by browning it in butter in a sauté pan.

POULET SAUTÉ
(WITH TWO VARIATIONS)

THE *POULET SAUTÉ* TECHNIQUE WAS FIRST DEFINED BY AUGUST Escoffier, the man who in the late nineteenth and early twentieth centuries codified classical French haute cuisine in *Le Guide Culinaire*. The chicken is browned on the stovetop (Escoffier would have used clarified butter, but vegetable oil will do the job), then finished in the oven. The pieces are removed from the pan, a sauce is made, and the chicken is reheated in the sauce. The *poulet sauté* also denotes a specific way of butchering a chicken that allows for easy preparation and elegant service—and gives the cook a carcass to prepare a stock in advance, which can be used to make pan sauce or *jus*.

After describing how to prepare the chicken for cooking—whole breast and wing drumettes removed in one piece, leg and thigh separated, thighbone removed—Escoffier lists more than 60 variations. I am offering my two favorites: a summer version that uses fresh tomatoes as the base for its sauce, and a great cold-weather version that features a milk-based sauce.

Step 1. Chicken breakdown for traditional poulet sauté: the whole breast, backbone removed, wing drumettes left on, drumsticks, and boned thighs; reserve wings, back, and thighbones for stock.

Step 2. All the pieces are browned.

Step 3. The thighs have been boned and the joint end of the drumstick has been removed for an elegant appearance.

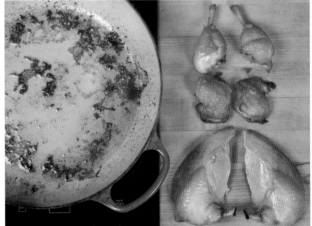

Step 4. Remove the chicken from the pan and prepare the sauce, then return the chicken to the pan to finish cooking it.

1 (3- to 4-pound/1.4- to 1.8-kilogram) chicken

Kosher salt

Vegetable oil or clarified butter

SERVES 2 TO 4

- **REMOVE** the wing tips and wing flats and **RESERVE** for stock; **LEAVE** the wing drumettes attached to the breast.

- To remove each leg from the body, **PLACE** the chicken breast-side up on your board. **CUT** between the leg and breast down to the joint where the leg connects to the carcass. **POP** the joint by pulling the leg out and away from the breast, then **CONTINUE** to slice through the skin to remove the leg. (There's a small muscle, part of the thigh, in an indentation in the backbone; **USE** your knife to capture this juicy nugget—it's known as the "oyster" for a reason!—rather than slicing through it and leaving it on the carcass.)

- To separate the thigh and drumstick, **PLACE** the leg skin-side down on your board. There's a thin line of fat running exactly above the joint; **FOLLOW** this line with your knife and your blade will slide right through the joint.

- With the thigh skin-side down, **RUN** your knife tip down the length of the thigh, right down the middle along the entire thighbone. **WORK** your knife around the sides of the bone to remove it from the muscle. **CUT** around either end of the thighbone to free it and all cartilage from the thigh meat; **RESERVE** the bone for stock. **REPEAT** with the other leg.

- With a knife or kitchen shears, **CUT** through the ribs connecting the breast to the backbone. **RESERVE** the back for stock.

- **PREHEAT** the oven to 425˚F/220˚C.

- **SEASON** the chicken with salt.

- In a low-sided sauté pan, **HEAT** the oil or clarified butter over medium-high heat. **LAY** the chicken pieces in the pan, skin-side down, and **BROWN** them. **FLIP** them, then **PLACE** the pan in the oven for 10 minutes. (The classicists out there may note that Escoffier puts a lid on the pan, but I find that this discourages good browning. I prefer to finish the cooking uncovered.) **REMOVE** the breast to a platter, then **RETURN** the pan to the oven to finish cooking the leg and thigh pieces, another 20 minutes or so.

- **REMOVE** each breast half by sliding a knife along either side of the keel bone, then slicing the breast from the rib cage. **SLICE** down through the joint where the wing bone connects to the carcass to keep it attached to the breast. **RESERVE** the carcass for stock.

- **REMOVE** the legs and thighs to prepare the sauce; **TRY** the variations on the following pages or make a simple pan sauce per the instructions on page 148.

Poulet Sauté
with Garlic, Basil, and Tomatoes

This is an excellent summer sauté, when basil and tomatoes are in season. The simple yet intensely flavored sauce takes advantage of the abundant liquid that salted tomatoes release.

2 tomatoes, diced

1 teaspoon kosher salt

1 chicken, prepared in the manner described on pages 61–62

5 garlic cloves, minced

¼ cup/60 grams butter

10 to 20 fresh basil leaves, cut into chiffonade

SERVES 2 TO 4

- At least 10 minutes before you're ready to prepare the sauce, **PUT** the tomatoes in a bowl and **SPRINKLE** them with the salt. **TOSS** them to distribute the salt after the first 5 minutes.

- When the chicken is done and removed to a platter, **POUR** off any excess fat and **ADD** the garlic. **SAUTE** the garlic over medium-high heat for 30 seconds or so.

- **POUR** the tomatoes and the liquid they've released into a mesh strainer or colander held over the pan so that only the tomato juices go into the pan. **USE** this liquid to deglaze the browned bits in the pan, scraping them up with a flat-edged wooden spoon. **WHISK** in the butter, then **ADD** the tomatoes and half of the basil. **RETURN** the chicken pieces to the pan and **SIMMER** gently to reheat them, 3 to 5 minutes. **SERVE** the chicken with the tomatoes and sauce spooned on top and garnished with the remaining basil.

Step 1. *Mise en place* for completing the *poulet sauté*: browned chicken, garlic, basil, butter, and chopped and salted tomatoes.

Step 2. Add the garlic to the pan and sauté until tender.

Step 3. Pour the tomatoes into a strainer over the pan, allowing all the tomato water to drain into the pan.

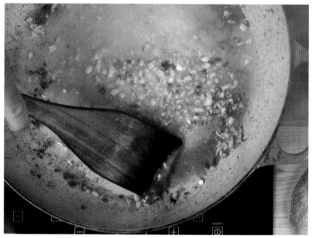

Step 4. The tomato water will deglaze the pan; scrape the browned bits using a flat-edged spatula as the tomato water reduces.

Step 5. Whisk the butter into the tomato water.

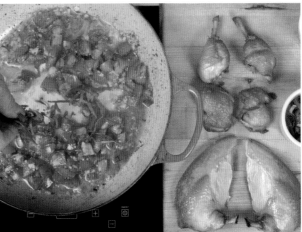

Step 6. Add the tomatoes and half of the julienned basil.

Step 7. Return the chicken to the pot to reheat it.

Poulet Sauté Stanley

I have to include this variation in honor of my dear friend and colleague Brian Polcyn, chef-owner of the Forest Grill outside Detroit and my coauthor for *Charcuterie* and *Salumi*. Covering the grueling Certified Master Chef exam for a magazine (a full account is in my book *The Soul of a Chef*), I found Brian to be the most engaging and edifying of the chefs I met. Twice during the test he was asked to cook a menu straight from Escoffier, and on his final day he drew the Poulet Sauté Stanley, which features a soubise sauce flavored with cayenne and curry. I include it here as a nod to the enduring friendship and collaboration with one of the finest chefs I know.

A classic *sauce soubise* is pureed until smooth; if you're going this route, then you can cut the onion any way you please. For a more rustic version of the sauce, begin with small-diced onion and leave the sauce as is. This sauce can also be used for just about any cut you might sauté.

1 chicken, prepared in the manner described on pages 61–62

1 medium onion, sliced or diced as desired (see headnote)

2 teaspoons curry powder

½ teaspoon cayenne pepper

½ cup/120 milliliters dry white wine

1 cup/240 milliliters Béchamel (page 160)

Kosher salt

Freshly ground black pepper

1 recipe Sautéed Mushrooms (page 19)

SERVES 4

- When the chicken is done and removed to a platter, **PLACE** the pan over medium-high heat and **ADD** the onion. **COOK**, stirring frequently, till translucent, 3 to 5 minutes. **ADD** the curry and cayenne. **STIR** to lightly toast the spices, then **DEGLAZE** the pan with the wine. **COOK** until the wine is almost gone, then **STIR** in the béchamel. If desired, **USE** a hand-held immersion blender to puree the sauce (or **PUREE** it in a countertop blender, then **RETURN** it to the pan). **TASTE** the sauce and **ADJUST** for seasoning. **RETURN** the chicken pieces to the pan to rewarm them in the sauce.

- To serve, **SPOON** the sauce over the chicken and **SERVE** with the sautéed mushrooms.

SAUTÉED DUCK BREASTS WITH RHUBARB "GASTRIQUE"

DUCK REMAINS ONE OF THE MOST OVERLOOKED MEATS, which is surprising given its great flavor and texture. It's most economical to buy duck whole, remove the breasts to sauté, render the remaining fat to confit the legs, and use the carcass, wings, and neck for stock.

One of the great pleasures of duck breast is the crispness you can bring to its skin. The challenge is that the skin, which is connective tissue made of protein, rides atop a thick layer of watery fat. The skin won't crisp until the water has cooked out of the fat, so the key is to use a low-temperature sauté. This low heat also makes it easy to cook the breast to the right temperature, medium rare. The meat side will stay raw while the fat renders; when the skin is almost perfectly done, turn the heat to high for a few minutes to finish crisping the skin, flip the breast, and let it cook for a minute more.

I like to serve this dish with an additional rhubarb garnish (see the box on page 72); while that is cooking, you can gently steam some spring onions to serve alongside.

2 duck breasts

Kosher salt

Freshly ground black pepper

1 teaspoon vegetable oil

1 recipe Rhubarb "Gastrique" (page 73)

Rhubarb garnish (optional; page 72)

SERVES 2

- **CROSSHATCH** the duck skin with a sharp knife, taking care not to cut all the way into the meat. **GIVE** the skin an aggressive layer of salt and **GRIND** some pepper over the meat side at least 10 minutes and up to 2 days before cooking (**PUT** the breasts in the refrigerator if they'll be sitting out for longer than an hour).

- **HEAT** the oil in a sauté pan over low heat. **LAY** the duck breasts in the pan, skin-side down, and **COOK** until the fat has rendered and the skin is brown and crisp, 15 to 20 minutes. Using a spatula, **PRESS** down on the breasts every now and then to squeeze the fat out.

- **TURN** the heat to high; after a few minutes, when the skin is perfect in your opinion, **FLIP** the breasts. **COOK** for another minute, just enough to color the meat. **REMOVE** the breasts to a cutting board and **ALLOW** to rest for 5 minutes.

- **SPREAD** a layer of gastrique on each plate. If you wish, **SLICE** the duck on the bias and **GARNISH** with the syrupy rhubarb slices.

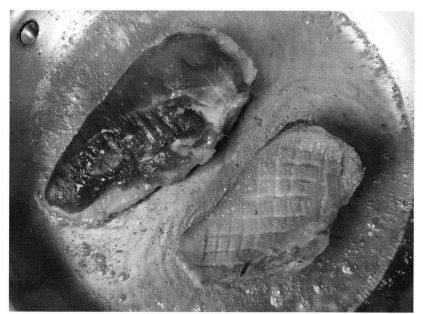

Step 1. Duck breasts are cooked skin-down over low heat to render the fat and water from the skin so that it can brown.

Step 2. The duck is flipped and quickly cooked on the other side until it's medium rare, then removed to a cutting board and sliced on the bias.

To Make the Optional Garnish

- **COMBINE** 1 cup water, 1 cup sugar, and the peel of 1 orange in a shallow pan and **BRING** to a simmer over medium heat. **ADD** 20 to 30 $1/2$-inch/12-millimeter slices of rhubarb (from 1 or 2 stalks), cut on the bias, to the orange simple syrup and **REDUCE** the heat to low. **COOK** the rhubarb until it is tender, 10 to 15 minutes. **STRAIN** and **GARNISH** the finished duck with the rhubarb slices.

(**NOTE** that the cooking liquid is delicious and can be added to gin or rum with some bitters to make a delicious cocktail.)

Rhubarb "Gastrique"

A gastrique is technically a sauce made by adding vinegar to caramelized sugar, but in contemporary cooking it can refer to almost any sweet-and-sour sauce accompanying a savory dish. Here, no acid is needed because the rhubarb is so tart. This is a lovely pairing with duck in the spring, when rhubarb comes into season.

2 tablespoons/30 grams butter

¼ cup/30 grams minced shallot

Kosher salt

2 cups/250 grams diced rhubarb (from 2 or 3 stalks)

2 tablespoons/30 grams sugar

2 tablespoons/30 grams honey

Ground cloves

Freshly grated nutmeg

Freshly ground black pepper

MAKES ABOUT 1 CUP/240 MILLILITERS

- In a small saucepan, **MELT** the butter over medium heat. **ADD** the shallot, **STIR** to coat with butter, and **HIT** it with a four-finger pinch of salt. When the shallot is translucent, **ADD** the rhubarb and **COOK**, stirring every now and then until the rhubarb begins to break down, about 5 minutes. **STIR** in the sugar and honey and **ADD** a small pinch of ground cloves, several gratings of nutmeg, and about 10 grinds of pepper. **REDUCE** the heat to medium-low and **COOK** until the rhubarb has become a thick sauce, 10 to 15 more minutes. **TASTE** and **ADJUST** the seasoning as desired.

VEAL MARSALA
WITH SAUTÉED MUSHROOMS

THIS VERSION OF SCALOPPINE, NOT UNLIKE THE ONE THAT opens the book, is an especially good, rich winter dish. It uses the sauce made from sautéed mushrooms and flavors it with Marsala, a fortified wine from Sicily. You can use any wine you wish of this style, including Madeira or a good sherry.

4 (5-ounce/150-gram) slices veal top round

Kosher salt

Freshly ground black pepper

Flour

2 tablespoons vegetable oil

1 to 2 tablespoons minced shallot

½ cup/120 milliliters Marsala wine

1 recipe Sautéed Mushrooms (page 19)

½ cup/120 milliliters half-and-half

SERVES 4

- If you'll be cooking the veal in batches, **PREHEAT** the oven to 200°F/95°C.

- **PLACE** each veal slice between two sheets of plastic wrap and **POUND** with a meat mallet or skillet to a thickness of about ¼ inch/5 millimeters. **SEASON** the scaloppine with salt and pepper.

- **PUT** enough flour for coating the veal on a plate—½ cup/70 grams or so.

- **SET** a large sauté pan over high heat. **DREDGE** the veal in the flour and **SHAKE** off all the excess. When the pan is hot, **ADD** the vegetable oil. **SWIRL** it around the pan until it's hot. **LOWER** the heat to medium-high and **LAY** two or four of the floured veal scaloppine in the hot oil, depending on the size of your pan—they should not be touching each other. **COOK** the veal till you've developed a nice browned crust, about 1 minute. **FLIP** the veal and **REPEAT** on the other side. If you're cooking the veal in batches, **HOLD** the cooked veal in the warm oven while you sauté the rest.

- When all the veal is done, **ADD** the shallots to the empty pan and **SAUTE** till they're heated through, 15 or 20 seconds. **ADD** the wine and **COOK**, scraping up any flour stuck to the pan, until the wine has reduced by two-thirds, then **ADD** the mushrooms and half-and-half. **BRING** to a simmer for a minute or two for the flavors to infuse the half-and-half.

- **RETURN** the veal to the pan to rewarm and coat each side with the sauce. **SERVE** immediately, spooning the mushrooms and sauce over the veal.

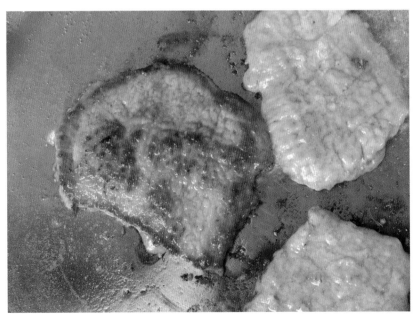

Step 1. Brown the pounded and floured meat.

Step 2. Sauté the shallots, then deglaze the pan with the wine.

Step 3. Use a flat-edged spatula to scrape up the browned bits.

Step 4. Add the mushrooms and half-and-half and cook till heated through.

Step 5. Cooking the mushrooms will further flavor the sauce.

Step 6. Return the veal to the pan to reheat, then serve.

SAUTÉED SWEET-BREADS
WITH SPINACH AND BACON

VEAL SWEETBREADS ARE NOT COMMONLY COOKED AT HOME; I'm offering this recipe in the hope that it might become less uncommon. A whole sweetbread—which is, in fact, the thymus gland of the cow—weighs about 1 pound/450 grams. The top lobe of the gland, called the "nut," is preferable for its shape and lack of membrane; the bottom lobe is long and tapering and contains more membrane. You can use either several nuts or one whole sweetbread for this recipe.

Sweetbreads should be soaked in lightly salted water overnight if possible to help leach out any remaining blood and to season the meat. Once they're blanched, cleaned, and chilled, they're ready to slice and sauté, and have a wonderful crispy exterior and a soft interior, with a mild flavor, here enhanced by the bacon. Because they're very rich, I pair them with sautéed spinach and finish it all with a few drops of balsamic vinegar.

Kosher salt

1 pound/450 grams sweetbreads

4 ounces/120 grams bacon, cut in strips

Flour

Vegetable oil

1½ pounds/675 grams spinach

Freshly ground black pepper

Balsamic vinegar

SERVES 4

- **FILL** a large pot with enough water to liberally cover the sweetbreads. **ADD** a tablespoon of salt and the sweetbreads. **BRING** the water to a boil over high heat, then **REDUCE** the heat to a simmer for 10 minutes. **REMOVE** the sweetbreads to an ice bath and **CHILL** completely.

- **REMOVE** as much membrane and fat as you can (anything that isn't clearly a part of this large gland). **PUT** the sweetbreads on a paper towel–lined plate, **COVER** with plastic, and **REFRIGERATE** for at least 2 hours or up to a day. (**SET** a light weight, such as a sauté pan or a couple of dinner plates, on the sweetbreads so that they have a uniform thickness.)

- **CUT** the sweetbreads into four equal portions—you can follow the natural seams or cut to your desired shape.

- **PREHEAT** your oven to 350°F/180°C.

- **PUT** a medium pan over medium-low heat and **SAUTE** the bacon until crisp. While the bacon cooks, **SEASON** the sweetbreads with salt and **DREDGE** them in flour. When the bacon is done, **TURN** the burner off and **STRAIN** all but a tablespoon of the rendered bacon fat into a clean sauté pan that can accommodate the sweetbreads.

- If necessary, **ADD** enough additional oil to the sauté pan with the bacon fat so that you have a good ¼-inch/5-millimeter depth. **ALLOW** the oil to get hot over high heat, then **REDUCE** the heat to medium-high and **ADD** the sweetbreads. **SAUTE** them on each side until they are beautifully golden brown, about 3 minutes per side, then **PUT** the pan in the oven for 15 minutes, turning the sweetbreads midway through (don't worry about overcooking them).

- Just before removing the sweetbreads from the oven, **REHEAT** the bacon till it's sizzling (adding a tablespoon of minced shallot wouldn't be out of line here), then **ADD** the spinach and **SAUTE** until it has collapsed and is hot, seasoning it to taste with salt and pepper. The liquid it releases will deglaze the pan of the bacon fond.

- **DIVIDE** the spinach and bacon among four plates. **DRIZZLE** each with about ½ teaspoon balsamic vinegar and **TOP** with a sweetbread. **SERVE** hot.

SAUTÉED
SHRIMP
WITH GARLIC-BUTTER SAUCE AND SAFFRON RICE PILAF

HERE IS A CLASSIC SAUTÉ: TENDER SHRIMP COOKED IN A small amount of oil, with a rich, garlicky sauce made in the same pan. Unlike sweetbreads or chicken thighs, which have a more generous window of doneness, shrimp can go from tender to rubbery in a New York minute. For optimal tenderness, it's important to just cook the shrimp through; the shrimp will finish cooking in the gentle heat of the sauce. Touch them along the way to gauge how quickly they cook; when they're done they should be firm but still have some give.

This dish teaches an *à la minute* technique—what is, in effect, a *beurre blanc* sauce: wine is partially cooked off, then whole butter is emulsified into it. If you choose to make stock from the shrimp shells, it also teaches, in chef's parlance, "total utilization" (in other words, using everything). This stock can be used to flavor rice to serve with the shrimp. Alternatively, you can make a plain rice pilaf, or simply steam white rice; the shrimp could also be served over pasta.

1½ pounds/675 grams shrimp (preferably U16/20),
peeled and deveined, shells reserved for stock if desired

1½ tablespoons minced garlic

1 to 2 tablespoons olive oil

Kosher salt

Freshly ground black pepper

1 tablespoon vegetable oil

½ cup/120 milliliters dry white wine

¼ cup/60 grams cold butter, cut into pieces

2 tablespoons minced fresh parsley

SERVES 4

- In a bowl, **COMBINE** the shrimp and garlic and **TOSS** with just enough olive oil to coat the shrimp. **SPRINKLE** with salt and pepper to taste—don't be shy!

- In a large sauté pan over high heat, **HEAT** the vegetable oil. When the oil is hot, **ADD** the shrimp; be sure to **GET** all the garlic into the pan as well. **COOK** until pink, about a minute. **FLIP** or **TOSS** the shrimp to cook their other sides.

- When they've taken on some color but are still soft in the center, **ADD** the wine, tossing the shrimp as it bubbles away. When about half of the wine has cooked off, 30 to 60 seconds, **ADD** the butter, swirling the pan continuously so that the butter emulsifies into the wine. When the butter is completely melted, **ADD** the parsley, **TOSS** the shrimp to distribute it, and **REMOVE** the pan from the heat.

- **SPOON** the butter sauce over the shrimp to serve.

Step 1. *Mise en place* for sautéed shrimp: shrimp and garlic, wine, butter, black pepper, parsley, kosher salt.

Step 2. Add the shrimp and garlic to the oil in a hot pan.

Step 3. When the shrimp are not quite cooked through, add the wine.

Step 4. After the wine has simmered and reduced, whisk in the butter; continue to whisk until the butter is completely emulsified into the sauce.

Step 5. Add the parsley just before serving.

Step 6. The shrimp has finished cooking in the sauce and is uniformly coated with sauce, garlic, and parsley.

Saffron Rice Pilaf

This simple rice pilaf is flavored with saffron and stock made from shrimp shells, and uses the classic pilaf technique: starting on the stovetop and finishing in the oven. Making a shellfish stock is, of course, an optional step and not something I'd do on a rushed weeknight. This is more manageable if you peel the shrimp and make the stock a day before you make the finished dish. Otherwise, you can simply make the pilaf with water.

FOR THE SHELLFISH STOCK:

2 teaspoons vegetable oil

1 shallot, thinly sliced

½ carrot, sliced with a peeler into ribbons

Kosher salt

Shells from at least 1 pound/450 grams shrimp

1 teaspoon tomato paste

3 tablespoons brandy

2 cups/480 milliliters water

2 or 3 fresh thyme sprigs (optional)

FOR THE PILAF:

1 tablespoon butter

1 small onion, cut into small dice (¼ cup/40 grams or so)

Kosher salt

1 cup/200 grams basmati or jasmine rice

¼ cup/40 grams orzo

⅛ teaspoon saffron threads

1 bay leaf

SERVES 4

TO MAKE THE SHELLFISH STOCK:

• In a medium saucepan, **HEAT** the vegetable oil over medium-high heat. When it's hot, **ADD** the shallot and carrot and **COOK** till they're tender, a few minutes, hitting them with a three-finger pinch of salt as you do. **ADD** the shells and **COOK**, stirring frequently, until the shells have turned pink. **ADD** the tomato paste and **CONTINUE** stirring to cook the paste. **ADD** the brandy to deglaze the pan, scraping the bottom clean with a flat-edged wooden spoon. **ADD** the water and the thyme (if using) and **BRING** the pot to a simmer, then **TURN** the heat to low and **COOK** for 20 to 30 minutes. **STRAIN** through a cloth or at least a fine-mesh strainer.

TO MAKE THE PILAF:

• **PREHEAT** your oven to 300°F/150°C.

• In a small saucepan, **MELT** the butter over medium-high heat, then **ADD** the onion and a four-finger pinch of salt. When the onion is soft (after a couple minutes), **ADD** the rice and orzo and **STIR** to toast the rice. **ADD** 1¾ cups/420 milliliters of the shellfish stock (if you don't have enough, add water), the saffron, and the bay leaf. As the stock comes up to a simmer, **TASTE** it. It should taste pleasantly seasoned (this is the seasoning level the finished rice will have); if it could use more salt, **ADD** it now.

• When it comes to a simmer, **COVER** the pan and **PLACE** it in the oven until all the liquid has been absorbed, 15 to 20 minutes. **SERVE** hot.

Step 1. Sauté the vegetables until tender, then add the shrimp shells and cook until they're pink.

Step 2. The tomato paste has been added and cooked, the pan has been deglazed with brandy, and water is added last.

Step 3. Cook the stock gently, preferably with thyme, for 20 to 30 minutes.

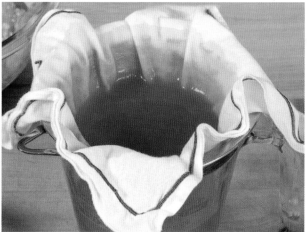

Step 4. Strain the finished stock through cloth.

SAUTÉED
FLOUNDER

THIS IS THE KIND OF PREPARATION THAT DOESN'T REALLY need a recipe—a quick and definitive sauté. Heat a bit of oil and butter in a nonstick sauté pan and cook the fish till it's just heated through. Finish with a little extra butter and serve with a squeeze of lemon and salt and pepper to taste. It's that simple.

Just about any flatfish will work. Check the Monterey Bay Aquarium Seafood Watch website for recommendations on which fish to choose, or buy from Whole Foods Market or other stores that use their own sustainability watch lists. If the fish is very thin, you may not even need to turn it; basting the top with hot butter will be enough to cook it through, as with the flounder shown here. Sautéed Asparagus (page 33) makes a fine accompaniment.

Step 1. After laying the fish in the hot pan, add the butter.

Step 2. These fillets will not be flipped because they're so thin, so cook the top by basting it with the hot butter.

Step 3. Serve, spooning the pan butter over the fish and, if you wish, garnish with freshly chopped parsley.

2 teaspoons vegetable oil

1 to 3 tablespoons/15 to 45 grams butter

4 flounder (or other lean flatfish) fillets

Fine sea salt

Freshly chopped parsley (optional)

4 lemon wedges

SERVES 4

- In a large sauté pan (preferably nonstick), **HEAT** the oil and 1 tablespoon of the butter over medium heat. Lightly **SEASON** the fish with the salt. When the butter is melted, **LAY** the fish in the pan and **COOK** for a minute or so. If the fish is thick, **FLIP** the fish and **CONTINUE** to cook, adding another tablespoon or two of butter, just until the fish is heated through, another minute or so. If the fish is thin, **ADD** the butter and **BASTE** continuously with a spoon until the flesh becomes opaque (the hot butter helps cook the fish evenly). **SERVE** immediately with lemon.

SAUTÉED
COD
WITH CLAMS

FOR A SERIOUSLY NEW ENGLAND MEAL, YOU CAN'T BEAT sautéed cod served on top of clam chowder that has been reduced to a thick, saucy consistency. (It's likely to be New England in style only, as Atlantic cod supplies have long been down. You'll probably find Alaskan or Icelandic cod at the fishmonger's.) Cod is an excellent fish to sauté, as you can get the oil hot enough to achieve a golden crust without overcooking the fish. A nice thick piece means you have some leeway in cooking it.

For this dish, sauté the chowder ingredients—smoky bacon, onion, potato—and add clams and a béchamel to create what will become the sauce. Canned clams are fine for this, but if you want to go all out, get a dozen or so quahogs, cook them in a couple cups of water, strain the liquid, and use that in the sauce along with the clams, chopped. The chowder base can be made ahead and reheated when needed. (If you have leftovers, thin it with a little wine or milk to turn it into a fabulous soup.)

2 bacon slices, minced

½ cup/120 milliliters water

1 medium onion, cut in small dice

Kosher salt

1 small potato (about 4 ounces/120 grams),
cut in small dice

½ cup/120 milliliters dry white wine,
plus more if needed

1 (10-ounce/283-gram) can baby clams, drained

1 recipe Béchamel (page 160)

12 littleneck clams (optional)

Vegetable oil

4 (6-ounce/180-gram) cod fillets

Fine sea salt

4 small thyme sprigs

SERVES 4

- **COMBINE** the bacon and water in a small saucepan over high heat. When the water has cooked off and the bacon is crackling, **LOWER** the heat to medium and **ADD** the onion, along with a pinch of kosher salt. **COOK** the onion over medium heat till soft. **ADD** the potato and **COOK** until nearly tender, then **ADD** the white wine, which will deglaze the pan, and finish cooking the potatoes, a few more minutes. **ADD** the clams to the pot. When the wine has nearly cooked off, **ADD** the béchamel and **BRING** to a simmer, then **KEEP** warm until you're ready to finish the dish.

- If using the littlenecks, **PUT** them in a small pan with an inch of water, **COVER**, and **COOK** over high heat until the clams open, a few minutes. **REMOVE** the pan from the heat but **KEEP** it covered.

- **HEAT** a ¼-inch/5-millimeter layer of oil in a sauté pan (preferably non-stick) over high heat. **SEASON** the cod fillets with sea salt. When the oil is very hot, just before it smokes, **LAY** the fillets in the pan. **COOK** until golden brown on the bottom, about 1 minute. **TURN** the cod and **CONTINUE** to cook until it's warm in the center, another minute. **TEST** the heat if you're uncertain; a cake tester or paring knife inserted into the center should feel warm, not cold, when you press it to the skin below your lower lip or the inside of your wrist. **REMOVE** to a plate lined with paper towels.

- To serve, **SPOON** some chowder onto each plate, **TOP** the chowder with the cod, and **GARNISH** each plate with 3 littleneck clams and a sprig of thyme.

Step 1. Bacon is sautéed and onion and potato are cooked in that rendered fat. Then the clams are added.

Step 2. When the clams are hot, béchamel sauce is added.

Step 3. The sauce is simmered briefly to allow the flavors to infuse it. It can be kept warm (or even refrigerated for a day or two), then reheated before serving.

SOFT-SHELL CRAB "LOUIS" SANDWICHES

SOFT-SHELL CRABS, WHICH CAN APPEAR AS EARLY AS APRIL and live on as late as September, are one of the great seasonal treats of the United States. Blue crabs along the Atlantic Seaboard begin to molt in spring, leaving their new exoskeletons soft and, when cooked, delightfully chewable. That unusual texture combines with the crab's flesh and mild, custard-like interior to make the soft-shell crab unlike anything else we eat.

It used to be that you could enjoy them only in certain seafood restaurants, but as American home cooks branch out into new territory, soft-shell crabs have become increasingly available at retail. It's best to buy them live and prepare them yourself. (You'll have to chop off the head and remove the lungs, which are always to be avoided in crabs and lobsters. It's easy to do, and there are plenty of video tutorials online.) For the squeamish, you can trust a place such as Whole Foods Market, which often carries them or will fill a special order, to prepare them for you the same day. They should smell of the fresh ocean; if they smell like low tide you're better off shopping elsewhere.

Once they're prepped, they're a breeze to cook. I coat them in a mixture of cornmeal and flour, then quickly sauté them and serve them on soft bread with rémoulade—a sophisticated sibling of tartar sauce. I've taken the spicy flavor of the sauce used for the classic 1960s dish Crab Louis and turned it into a sandwich condiment, with sriracha sauce giving heat to the rémoulade. You could also just add minced chipotle peppers in adobo sauce or Old Bay Seasoning to mayonnaise. It's up to you.

1 recipe Rémoulade (page 152)

1½ teaspoons sriracha sauce

1 cup/70 grams shredded iceberg lettuce

½ cup/10 grams arugula

4 thin tomato slices, lightly salted

8 slices soft bread, toasted if desired

½ cup/70 grams flour

½ cup/75 grams cornmeal

Kosher salt

4 soft-shell crabs, cleaned

Vegetable oil

SERVES 4

- **COMBINE** the rémoulade and sriracha and **STIR** till uniformly mixed. **SET** aside. Also **GET** the lettuce, arugula, tomato, and bread ready before beginning the crab.

- **COMBINE** the flour and cornmeal in a shallow dish. **SALT** the crabs and **DREDGE** them in the mixture.

- **POUR** vegetable oil into a large sauté pan to a depth of ¼ inch/5 millimeters and heat over high heat. When the oil is hot, **LAY** the crabs in, belly up. (They cook quickly, so you can do them in batches of two if you don't have room for all four at once.) **REDUCE** the heat to medium-high and **COOK** for 60 to 90 seconds per side. They should have a nice browned crust and be cooked all the way through. **REMOVE** the crabs to a plate lined with paper towels to drain.

- **COMPOSE** your sandwiches and **EAT** immediately.

Step 1. Soft-shell crabs ready to bread and cook.

Step 2. Dredge the crabs in the flour-cornmeal mixture.

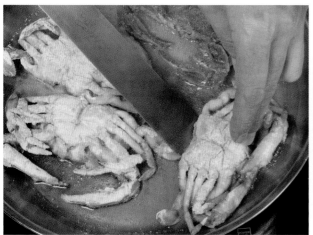

Step 3. Sauté the crabs belly up until they're nicely seared.

Step 4. Brown the bellies to finish, then serve immediately.

SAUTÉED **PORK CHOPS** WITH SAUCE ROBERT

NOTHING COULD BE SIMPLER OR MORE DELICIOUS THAN quickly sautéed pork chops finished in the oven. But because this sauté doesn't result in a sauce as a by-product of the cooking, you must make the sauce separately. I've chosen a classic sauce Robert, one of the oldest French sauces on record. With its mustardy tang, it's a delicious accompaniment to pork. This was the first traditional sauce I was taught to make, and I love it for that reason as well. In culinary school we started with a brown "mother sauce" made of veal stock and thickened with roux. Here I use stock only and thicken it with *beurre manié*, which is flour kneaded into butter. The butter coats the granules of flour so they don't clump as they expand to thicken the sauce, and the butter enriches the sauce. You can use veal, pork, or even chicken stock. Because it's reduced, I don't recommend store-bought broths, but if you must go that route, use a heavier hand with the mustard—my go-to brand is Maille.

4 thick pork chops
(order them from your butcher cut 1¼ inches/3 centimeters thick)

Kosher salt

Freshly ground black pepper

Flour

Vegetable oil

2 teaspoons minced fresh parsley

FOR THE SAUCE:

1 tablespoon butter

2 tablespoons minced shallot

½ cup/120 milliliters dry white wine

Freshly ground black pepper

¾ cup/180 milliliters pork or veal stock

1 tablespoon Dijon mustard

Squeeze of lemon juice (about 1 teaspoon)

1 to 2 teaspoons beurre manié
(2 teaspoons flour kneaded with a fork or by hand
into 2 teaspoons softened butter)

SERVES 4

TO MAKE THE PORK CHOPS:

- **REMOVE** the chops from the refrigerator 1 to 2 hours before cooking them. **SALT** them so that they have an even coating of salt on both sides. **GRIND** pepper over them.

- **PREHEAT** your oven to 325°F/165°C.

- **DREDGE** the pork chops in flour and **PAT** them so all the excess flour falls off. **HEAT** a large sauté pan over medium-high heat (**USE** two pans or **DO** them in batches if you don't have a big enough pan). **POUR** in enough oil to make a layer about ⅛ inch/3 millimeters deep. When the oil is hot, **LAY** the pork chops in it and **COOK** until they're golden brown, 2 to 3 minutes. **TURN** them and **BROWN** the other side, another 2 to 3 minutes.

- **REMOVE** them to a separate pan or a baking sheet and **HOLD** them in the oven to finish cooking while you make the sauce (they should be in the oven for 5 to 10 minutes).

TO MAKE THE SAUCE:

- **POUR** off all the oil from the sauté pan. If any of the fond (the browned bits sticking to the bottom of the pan) has burned, **CLEAN** the pan completely. Otherwise, **LEAVE** it in to give flavor to the sauce.

- **MELT** the butter over medium heat. **ADD** the shallot and cook till translucent. **ADD** the wine, **TURN** the burner to high, and **ALLOW** the wine to boil off. **ADD** plenty of freshly cracked pepper, 10 grindings or so. When almost all the wine has cooked off (there will be liquid bubbling, but the shallot should be sticking out of it), **ADD** the stock. **BRING** it to a simmer and **REDUCE** it by about one-third. **WHISK** in the mustard and lemon. **ADD** enough *beurre manié* to thicken the sauce as desired. **TASTE** for seasoning; I find that the mustard obviates the need for more salt, but use your senses.

- **REMOVE** the pork chops from the oven (their internal temperature should be around 135°F/55°C). **SPOON** the sauce over them, **SPRINKLE** with minced parsley, and **SERVE**.

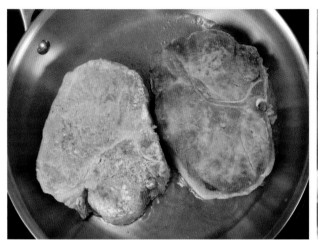

Step 1. Sauté the chops until they're beautifully browned on each side, then place them in the oven while you make the sauce in the sauté pan.

Step 2. Sauce *mise en place*: lemon, stock, wine, shallots, mustard, and beurre manié.

Step 3. Sauté the shallots until they're tender.

Step 4. Add the wine and cook till it's almost evaporated.

Step 5. Add the stock and begin reducing the sauce.

Step 6. While the stock reduces, add the mustard.

Step 7. Whisk in the beurre manié until it's completely melted, then season with lemon.

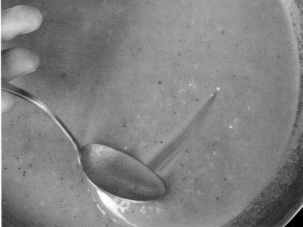
Step 8. Cook until the sauce reaches the consistency you desire.

CHICKEN-FRIED STEAK

WITH ONION GRAVY

I HAPPENED TO BE LISTENING TO THE AUDIO VERSION OF Molly Wizenberg's engaging memoir *Delancey*, about opening a restaurant in Seattle, when she mentioned chicken-fried steak as being her native Oklahoma's state dish, along with okra and black-eyed peas. Suddenly I grew hungry for this splendid three-part meal.

Chicken-fried steak falls into the "Why don't I make this more often?" category. And that's why I'm including it here: because I should, and *you* should, make this on a regular basis. It's immensely satisfying to eat, and it represents the best of what home cooking really is: taking an inexpensive, fairly bland cut of meat and, using your knowledge and skills as a cook, elevating this lowly cut to excellence—to the point that it's so good, you ask yourself, "Why don't I make this more often?"

Just the sound of it is appealing in its seeming decadence—*chicken-fried steak*. And yet it's not really that decadent at all, even with the onion gravy I like to serve with it. I use a very lean cut of beef and sauté it in vegetable oil. Nutritious and delicious.

Traditionally, chicken-fried steak uses the same flour-buttermilk-flour dipping method used for fried chicken, but I find that the flour becomes mushy by the time it reaches the table. Instead I use panko for the final coating so that it stays crispy.

FOR THE GRAVY:

1 teaspoon vegetable oil

½ onion, cut in small dice

Kosher salt

1 cup Béchamel (page 160)

¼ teaspoon cayenne pepper (optional)

FOR THE STEAK:

4 (4- to 6-ounce/120- to 180-gram) pieces of
beef top or bottom round

Kosher salt

1 tablespoon freshly ground black pepper,
plus more for seasoning the meat

2 tablespoons flour

1 tablespoon paprika (hot or sweet, your preference)

1 tablespoon chili powder

1 teaspoon cayenne pepper
(consider halving this if your paprika is very hot)

2 eggs

1 cup/240 milliliters buttermilk

2 cups/135 grams panko

Vegetable oil

Minced fresh parsley (optional)

SERVES 4

TO MAKE THE GRAVY:

- **HEAT** the oil in a small saucepan over medium-high heat, then **ADD** the onion. **GIVE** the onion a three-finger pinch of salt and **COOK** at least till the onion is softened. For a deeper, sweeter flavor, **COOK** the onion till it's browned.

- When the onion is cooked as you wish, **ADD** the béchamel and **STIR** in the cayenne, if using. **BRING** to a simmer, then **COVER** and **REMOVE** from the heat. **KEEP** the gravy warm till you're ready to serve.

TO MAKE THE STEAK:

- **PREHEAT** the oven to 200°F/95°C.

- **SEASON** the meat with salt and pepper at least 10 minutes before cooking it.

- In a shallow dish, **COMBINE** the flour, 1 tablespoon black pepper, the paprika, chili powder, and cayenne until all the ingredients are evenly dispersed.

- In a separate dish, **BEAT** the eggs until uniform, then **WHISK** in the buttermilk. **SPREAD** the panko in a third dish.

- **PUT** each piece of meat between sheets of plastic wrap and **POUND** them with a meat mallet if you have one (I use the teeth side) or a skillet to tenderize and flatten them—the more surface area in the beginning, the more crispy goodness in the end. They should be no thicker than ½ inch/12 millimeters.

- **COAT** all sides of the meat with the seasoned flour mixture so that the entire surface is dry. **DIP** each piece into the buttermilk mixture, then into the panko.

- In a large sauté pan, **HEAT** about ⅜ inch/10 millimeters oil over medium-high heat. When it's rippling from the heat, **LAY** the steak pieces in the pan and **COOK** until they're golden brown, about 2 minutes per side.

- **COOK** them in batches if your pan is not big enough to hold all four pieces at once; **TRANSFER** each cooked piece to the warm oven while you finish the meal.

- **SERVE** topped with onion gravy and, if you wish, garnished with fresh parsley.

Sautéed Black-Eyed Peas and Okra

Black-eyed peas are high in protein, fiber, and other nutrients; given their low cost, they are among our most valuable foods. Most dried beans benefit from being soaked overnight before cooking, but black-eyed peas don't require this step. They'll cook relatively quickly—an hour or two at most. Remember that the more flavorful the cooking liquid, the more flavorful the beans, so I usually add aromatic vegetables and some bay leaves to the water. If you think of it, reserve $1/2$ cup/120 milliliters of the cooking liquid; you can add it to the sautéing peas to help heat them through.

Okra is an underused plant where I live in the eastern Midwest, but in summertime I'll often find fresh okra at our farmers' market and never hesitate to buy a pint or two. If cooked beyond a couple of minutes it will break down into what is often described as a "mucilaginous goo," and this is exactly as disgusting as it sounds. Cooked further, as in a gumbo, it will break down altogether and thicken the liquid it's cooking in. Here, the okra is sliced into discs and sautéed in oil (or clarified butter, which slightly enhances its flavor) for no more than a minute, just to heat it through. The okra doesn't need any more seasoning than salt and pepper, although you could spice it up with red pepper flakes. This is not only the easiest way to cook this underappreciated vegetable, it's the best way.

Together, black-eyed peas and okra make an excellent side dish—or a great stand-alone vegetarian meal.

4 tablespoons/60 milliliters olive oil or melted butter

½ diced onion

1 teaspoon whole cumin seeds or ground cumin

3 cups/500 grams cooked black-eyed peas
(reserve ½ cup/120 milliliters of the cooking liquid
if you think of it)

2 teaspoons white wine vinegar

Kosher salt

Freshly ground black pepper

1 to 2 teaspoons red pepper flakes (optional)

1 pound/450 grams okra,
cut into ½-inch/12-millimeter rounds

SERVES 4

- In a large sauté pan, **HEAT** 2 tablespoons of the olive oil over medium-high heat. **ADD** the onion and **COOK** until tender, 2 to 3 minutes. **ADD** the cumin and **COOK** for another 30 seconds. When hot, **ADD** the peas, jumping them until they are heated through. **ADD** the reserved cooking liquid or a little water so that they're moist; most of it will cook off. **SEASON** with the vinegar, **ADD** salt and pepper to taste, and **TRANSFER** to a serving dish.
- In the same pan, **HEAT** the remaining 2 tablespoons olive oil over high heat. When it's ripplingly hot, **ADD** the red pepper flakes (if using), then the okra, and **SHAKE** the pan to coat the okra with the fat. **JUMP** them or **STIR** frequently until they are heated through, a minute or so (**TASTE** one— it should still have some bite). **SEASON** with salt to taste.
- **TOP** the black-eyed peas with the okra and **SERVE.**

Step 1. Sauté the onion till tender, then add the cumin and let that cook briefly.

Step 2. Sauté the onion and cumin till they're well combined.

Step 3. Add the black-eyed peas.

Step 4. Sauté it all, jumping it in the pan till everything is combined.

Step 5. Add the melted butter to the hot pan (notice that the milky solids and water have sunk to the bottom).

Step 6. When the butter is hot, add the okra and season with salt.

Step 7. Sauté the okra just till heated through.

Step 8. Add the red pepper flakes, if using, toss to combine, and serve immediately, along with the black-eyed peas.

FLATIRON STEAK

WITH SAUTÉED SHALLOTS AND TARRAGON BUTTER

I'M OFTEN ASKED WHAT MY CHOICE WOULD BE FOR MY LAST meal. It begins with a couple dozen oysters and a bottle of dry sparkling wine, followed by *steak-frites* and a monster zinfandel. I maintain that since none of us knows when, as Brendan Gill once put it, "the inevitable catastrophe of death" will strike, one's last meal should be accessible so that you can have a reliable and frequent pleasure in this vale of tears. Good thing *steak-frites* is a simple bistro staple that's easy to make at home.

It is also a quintessential sauté: high heat applied to a piece of meat that doesn't need more tenderizing than with knife and fork at the table, with a sauce prepared in the pan while the meat rests. I recommend the flatiron, a relatively tough and inexpensive cut from the shoulder. It is deeply flavored, with notes of iron and liver, and immensely satisfying.

Here, shallots serve as the sauce, enriched and flavored with a compound butter—butter to which aromatics have been mixed in—while the beef rests. Serve this dish with French fries or sautéed spinach (page 29). Or both.

4 (6-ounce/180-gram) flatiron steaks

Kosher salt

Freshly ground black pepper

1 tablespoon vegetable oil

4 medium to large shallots, minced

½ cup/120 milliliters dry white wine

4 tablespoons/60 grams Tarragon Butter (page 164)

SERVES 4

- **TAKE** the steaks out of the refrigerator about 2 hours before you cook them. **GIVE** them an aggressive salting. **COVER** with plastic.

- **PUT** a large sauté pan or cast-iron skillet over high heat. **UNCOVER** the steaks and **BLOT** their surface dry with a paper towel. **GRIND** pepper over both sides of each steak. When the pan is good and hot, **ADD** the oil. It should ripple on contact. **SWIRL** it around the pan. **LAY** each steak in and **COOK** until a good sear is achieved, 1½ to 2 minutes. **FLIP** them and **CONTINUE** to cook to your desired doneness, another couple of minutes for rare (120°F/50°C). **REMOVE** to a board or platter to rest for at least 3 minutes.

- **LOWER** the heat to medium-high, **ADD** the shallots to the pan, and **STIR** with a flat-edged wooden spoon. **ADD** a three-finger pinch of salt. **CONTINUE** to stir them. When they have softened and browned, about a minute, **ADD** the wine. **CONTINUE** to cook until the wine has vaporized, stirring all the while. When the wine has cooked off, **TURN** the heat to medium-low until you're ready to serve.

- **SERVE** the steaks topped with the shallots and tarragon butter.

To Turn This into
Steak au Poivre

- **COAT** all sides of the steaks with a thick layer of coarsely ground black pepper and **COOK** as on page 124. While the steaks rest, **COOK** the shallots as on page 124. **DEGLAZE** with $1/2$ cup/120 milliliters brandy, then **ADD** $1/2$ cup/120 milliliters cream and **REDUCE** for a minute or two. **SERVE** the steaks with the shallots and tarragon butter.

STIR-FRIED
BEEF
WITH CELERY
AND CARROTS

THIS VERY SPICY STIR-FRY IS A VARIANT OF A RECIPE I'VE
been making since reading it in *The Chinese Cookbook* by Craig Claiborne and
Virginia Lee (written in 1972 and still a useful resource). I've enhanced the
dish with what I call the "Asian mirepoix" of ginger-garlic-scallions, but the
basic pairing of beef with celery and carrots is a humble yet exquisite combination—one that works for any beef (or venison) preparation, regardless of
the style of dish.

This dish incorporates both deep-frying and stir-frying to quickly cook
naturally tender ingredients. The stir-fry is the highest-heat and fastest sauté
there is. Many home kitchens don't have the heating power to get the pan hot
enough for true stir-fries, but if you use a heavy-gauge pan or heavy wok, and
let it get scorching hot before adding the oil, you can come close. Then let the
oil get almost smoking hot before adding the vegetables. Deep-frying delivers
a similar effect for the meat, enhancing the flavor of the beef by browning it
and crisping the edges.

This recipe is best using skirt steak, but you can also use flank steak—it
just takes a little more cutting to turn slices of flank steak into strips. Use a
mandoline to julienne the vegetables, if you have one.

2 tablespoons soy sauce

2 tablespoons black soy sauce or tamari

2 tablespoons dry white wine, dry sherry, or Chinese rice wine

1 teaspoon Asian fish sauce

1 teaspoon sugar

1 pound/450 grams skirt steak or flank steak

Kosher salt

1 cup/240 milliliters vegetable oil

6 to 12 dried red chiles

3 scallions, thinly sliced on the bias

1 (1-inch/2.5-centimeter) knob of ginger, grated

3 garlic cloves, smashed with the flat side of a knife

2 large carrots, julienned

2 celery ribs, julienned

SERVES 4

- In a small bowl, **WHISK** together the soy sauces, wine, fish sauce, and sugar and **SET** aside.

- **SLICE** the steak into ⅜-inch/10-millimeter strips and **SEASON** with salt.

- **BRING** the oil to about 375°F/190°C in a wok or large, heavy saucepan set over high heat. **ADD** the meat and **COOK**, stirring to separate the pieces, till thoroughly browned, 3 minutes or so. **REMOVE** the meat to a plate lined with paper towels. **POUR** off all but a tablespoon or two of the oil.

- **RETURN** the wok or pan to high heat. **ADD** the dried chiles and **STIR-FRY** till they're black (**TURN** on your exhaust hood if you have one!), 30 to 45 seconds. **ADD** the scallions, ginger, and garlic and **STIR-FRY** until softened, another 30 to 45 seconds. **ADD** the carrots and celery and **STIR-FRY** until tender, about 60 seconds. **RETURN** the cooked beef to the wok or pan, **ADD** the sauce, and **STIR-FRY** till everything is heated through and tender. **SERVE** immediately.

Step 1. Strips of beef are first deep-fried until they're well done but not dried out.

Step 2. Dried red chiles are stir-fried till black; they're very hot but also have a delicious, nutty flavor.

Step 3. Asian mirepoix—garlic, scallions, ginger—is the beginning of many great stir-fry dishes.

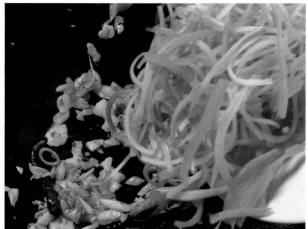

Step 4. Add the carrots and celery and stir-fry.

Step 5. Return the beef to the wok.

Step 6. Add the sauce, stir-fry, and serve immediately.

KEFTEDES
WITH TZATZIKI (AND THE SYMON SAYS BURGER)

I INCLUDE THIS DISH AS HOMAGE TO CLEVELAND CHEF Michael Symon, from whom I have learned so much about big flavors and specific dishes, such as lamb meatballs and yogurt sauce, both reflecting his Greek heritage. While I tinker with his recipe slightly, I don't vary the cinnamon. It's easy to go overboard with this powerful spice, but when used in the proper proportion it's what gives these meatballs their beguiling note.

Olive oil

1 shallot, minced

½ cup/20 grams diced bread, day-old or toasted till dry

¼ cup/60 milliliters milk

1 pound/450 grams ground lamb

1 egg, well beaten

1 teaspoon minced garlic

2 teaspoons minced fresh oregano

1 teaspoon kosher salt

1 teaspoon ground coriander

½ teaspoon ground cumin

⅛ teaspoon ground cinnamon

1 cup/150 grams flour

1 tablespoon freshly ground black pepper

Freshly grated lemon zest, for garnish

Minced fresh mint, for garnish

1 recipe Tzatziki (page 167)

SERVES 4

- In a small saucepan, **HEAT** 1 tablespoon olive oil over medium-high heat. **SAUTE** the shallot until tender, a minute or two. **REMOVE** from the heat and **ALLOW** to cool.

- In a small bowl, **COMBINE** the bread and milk and **SET** aside to soak until the bread is soft.

- In a large bowl, **COMBINE** the shallot, soaked bread, lamb, egg, garlic, oregano, salt, coriander, cumin, and cinnamon and **MIX** by hand till all ingredients are uniformly distributed. **FORM** the mixture into balls the size of ping-pong balls.

- In a shallow dish, **WHISK** the flour and pepper till uniformly combined. **ROLL** the meatballs in this flour mixture.

- In a large sauté pan, **HEAT** about ¼ inch/5 millimeters oil over medium-high heat. When the oil is hot, **ADD** the meatballs and **SAUTE** them till all sides are golden brown, about 10 minutes. They should still have some squish to them when you squeeze them; remember that they'll keep cooking after you take them out of the pan.

- **SPRINKLE** lemon zest and mint over the meatballs and **SERVE** with the tzatziki.

To Turn This into the Symon Says Burger

- **FOLLOW** the keftedes recipe, but **INCREASE** all the ingredients for the lamb mixture by half again. **FORM** the mixture into four 6-ounce/170-gram patties. **DREDGE** the burgers in the seasoned flour, patting off any excess. In a large sauté pan or cast-iron pan, **HEAT** about 1/2 inch/10 millimeters olive oil over medium-high heat. When the oil is hot, **ADD** the burgers and **SAUTE** them till both sides are golden brown, about 10 minutes total. This will yield burgers that are between medium rare and medium; they should still have some give when you poke them, but they shouldn't feel squishy.

- **GRATE** lemon zest over the burgers and **SERVE** on English muffins. (This is another Michael Symon-inspired idea. We both highly recommend using Bays English muffins, by far the most flavorful on the market. They are usually located in the refrigerated aisle of your grocery store.) **TOP** with tzatziki, lettuce, and tomato in honor of Cleveland's best-known chef—after Chef Boyardee, that is.

SAUTÉED VENISON WITH CUMBERLAND SAUCE

IF YOU ARE A HUNTER OR KNOW SOMEONE WHO IS, YOU'RE sure to have some venison come into your life once a year. But deer meat is increasingly available year-round at specialty markets and by mail order. It's a rich, delicious meat, best cooked like beef. Venison loin is also perfect for a sauté. If you've left the meat out at room temperature for an hour or two, cooking it to a perfect medium rare is easy, as most of the cooking takes place while the venison rests and you make your pan sauce. I usually serve this with Fava Bean Succotash (page 41), but Sautéed Carrots and Celery (page 37) would also go well.

1½ pounds/675 grams venison loin

Kosher salt

Freshly ground black pepper

2 teaspoons vegetable oil or as needed

1 recipe Cumberland Sauce (page 154)

SERVES 4

- An hour or two before you're ready to start cooking, **TIE** the loin with butcher's twine to create a uniform cylinder, and **SALT** and **PEPPER** the meat. **LEAVE** it out at room temperature.

- **PLACE** a sauté pan over high heat. When the pan is hot, **ADD** the vegetable oil and **SWIRL** it around the pan. **ADD** the venison loin and **SEAR** it on all sides, 5 to 6 minutes in all, then **REMOVE** it to a cutting board to rest while you make the sauce. The heat will slowly penetrate to the center, giving you a uniform medium rare (about 125°F/52°C).

- **REMOVE** the string, **SLICE** into medallions, and **SERVE** with the sauce.

SAUTÉED
APPLE
STREUSEL,
SKILLET STYLE

WHEN I'M ENTERTAINING, I SPEND MOST OF MY TIME COOKING
the main course and side dishes, so when I get around to dessert, I want
something simple and fast. I created this streusel to be sautéed quickly on
the stovetop and finished under the broiler. Rather than baking fruit with a
streusel topping, I sauté both the fruit and the streusel topping so that they
take on a roasted flavor, then combine the two and broil to cook the sugar and
brown the top. This is so fast you can even make it after dinner if you have the
streusel topping pre-mixed. Ten minutes from stove to table—a warm, soulful
dessert, especially delicious à la mode.

2 tablespoons/30 grams butter

2½ to 3 pounds/1.13 to 1.36 kilograms Granny Smith apples,
peeled and thinly sliced (you should end up
with 1½ pounds/675 grams peeled sliced apples)

2 tablespoons granulated sugar

½ teaspoon ground cinnamon

¼ teaspoon ground cloves

FOR THE STREUSEL:

1 cup/90 grams rolled oats

½ cup/75 grams whole-wheat flour

½ cup/75 grams almond flour

½ cup/100 grams brown sugar

½ cup/120 grams butter, at room temperature

Vanilla ice cream (optional)

SERVES 6 TO 8

TO MAKE THE APPLES:

- In an 8-inch oven-safe skillet, **MELT** the butter over medium-high heat and **ADD** the apples, stirring to sauté them. **ADD** the granulated sugar. **SPRINKLE** the cinnamon and cloves evenly over the surface. **CONTINUE** to sauté, stirring now and then as the apples release moisture, till they are browned and collapsed but still have some bite, about 15 minutes.

- **PREHEAT** your broiler.

TO MAKE THE STREUSEL:

- In a large sauté pan, **COMBINE** the oats, whole-wheat flour, almond flour, and brown sugar over medium to medium-high heat. **STIR** this dry mixture to toast it all (even this is a form of sauté!). **CONTINUE** stirring until the mixture has a toasted aroma, 5 to 8 minutes.

- **ADD** the butter and **STIR** until the butter has melted and the streusel is entirely dampened by the butter.

- **POUR** the streusel over the apples and **PRESS** it down evenly to cover the surface of the apples. **PLACE** the skillet beneath the broiler until the streusel topping is browned, 3 to 5 minutes depending on your broiler.

- **ALLOW** to cool for 10 minutes if serving warm, or **COOL** completely.

- If you wish, **SERVE** topped with vanilla ice cream.

Step 1. Sautéed apples with spices begin this stovetop dessert.

Step 2. The apples are cooked until tender but not collapsed.

Step 3. The streusel topping is sautéed in a dry pan to toast the ingredients.

Step 4. Butter is added to bring the topping together.

Step 5. When the apples are done, top them with the streusel.

Step 6. The apple streusel is broiled briefly to brown the topping and finish cooking the streusel.

SAUCES FOR
SAUTÉS

SAUCES TEND TO GET SHORT SHRIFT IN THE HOME KITCHEN, yet they can elevate a dish to degrees that more than make up for the extra steps it takes to make one. We use store-bought sauces all the time to add flavor and satisfaction to many of our staple dishes: mustard and mayo for a sandwich, for instance. My kids wouldn't think of eating French fries without some kind of sauce; it used to be ketchup, but now my son has taken to requesting aioli, bless him. Sauces add flavor, moisture, and richness to food.

The sauté technique doesn't create a sauce as a by-product of cooking, as braising does, and the cooking time is not as long as it is with roasting, during which juices from the meat collect and reduce on the bottom of the pan. Yet sauces are an important element we don't want to ignore. Sauce not only completes a dish—sometimes it *makes* the dish. A good sauce is well worth the effort.

The following recipes address the three main strategies to create sauces for sautéed items: (1) make a quick pan sauce in the same pan you cooked the food in, (2) use a mother sauce, such as béchamel, which becomes your base, or (3) create a finished sauce from ingredients separate from the sauté ingredients, as with rémoulade and tzatziki.

BASIC PAN SAUCE

A quick sauce made in the same pan you cooked your main course in can be as simple as deglazing the pan with wine and swirling in a little butter. Add some chopped fresh herbs and you've doubled the power of the sauce.

If you have homemade stock on hand, an even richer and more complex sauce is a snap. I'm less quick to recommend store-bought stocks for pan sauces unless they are excellent. Many canned and boxed broths are laden with additives you wouldn't use if you were making the broth yourself; when you reduce that kind of liquid, you concentrate the bad qualities of the stock. See the box on page 151 for a quick alternative to packaged stock.

One reason we make pan sauces is that they are a way to avoid leaving any flavor in your sauté pan. The process of sautéing often leaves browned protein bits—juices that have been squeezed out of the meat and reduced to sticky, intensely flavored solids—in your sauté pan. If you've floured your meat, that flour may be browned as well and will even help thicken the sauce to some degree. When you add liquid to such a pan, the liquid loosens the browned bits so that the bottom of the pan can be scraped clean. The liquid itself (wine, stock, a vegetable juice such as tomato water), as well as any aromatic vegetables you may want to include, adds even more flavor. That's what you're looking for in a sauce. What I reach for first in the aromatic category is a shallot, which makes just about any savory preparation better. Finishing with fresh herbs almost always benefits the dish.

The last element of a pan sauce is its consistency. A *jus*, in which stock is flavored and reduced, is typically left thin. But sauce that's too thin won't stick to the food; you almost always want some kind of viscosity. To thicken small amounts of liquid, you can add flour to the pan before the liquid is added, cooking it briefly in the fat, or add the flour in the form of *beurre manié*, flour kneaded into some butter. Both techniques work by coating the flour granules in fat so that they don't adhere and create lumps. You can also use a cornstarch slurry, which is equal parts water and cornstarch mixed to the consistency of heavy cream. Cornstarch doesn't bind to itself in water as flour does, so water is all you need to evenly distribute the starch.

The following two methods offer quick, *à la minute* pan sauces—one wine-based, one stock-based. They can be used for virtually any meat or fish you sauté; the wine-based sauce, which is more acidic, is best with chicken and fish, the stock-based sauce with pork, veal, and beef.

All-Purpose Wine-Based Pan Sauce

1 tablespoon minced shallot

½ cup/120 milliliters dry white wine

¼ cup/60 grams cold butter, cut into several pieces

1 tablespoon minced fresh parsley

- When you have removed the sautéed meat or fish from the pan, **POUR** off any oil remaining in the pan and **RETURN** it to the burner over medium heat. **ADD** the shallot and **STIR** briefly to soften it. **ADD** the wine and **SCRAPE** up any of the browned bits stuck to the pan. When half of the wine has cooked off, **ADD** the butter and **SWIRL** the pan continuously until all the butter has melted. If you feel the sauce is too thin, **THICKEN** it slightly with *beurre manié* or a slurry as noted on page 149. **TURN** the flame to low and **ADD** the parsley or other optional flavorings (see the box on page 151).

All-Purpose Stock-Based Pan Sauce

1 tablespoon minced shallot

¼ cup/60 milliliters dry white wine

¾ cup/180 milliliters stock
(chicken, vegetable, pork, veal, beef, or fish)

1 tablespoon flour kneaded into 2 tablespoons softened butter

- When you have removed the sautéed meat or fish from the pan, **POUR** off any oil remaining in the pan and **RETURN** it to the burner over medium heat. **ADD** the shallot and **STIR** briefly to soften. **ADD** the wine and **SCRAPE** up any of the browned bits stuck to the pan. When most of the wine has cooked off, **ADD** the stock and **REDUCE** by about half. **ADD** the flour-butter mixture and **SWIRL** the pan continuously until all the butter has melted and the sauce has thickened. **TURN** the flame to low and **ADD** any optional flavorings (see the box on page 151).

Quick Ways to Enhance
a Basic Pan Sauce

Add fresh soft herbs—chopped parsley, chives, tarragon, or chervil or whole thyme leaves—just before serving.
Add chopped capers.
Season with a squeeze of fresh lemon juice.
Add cracked black pepper along with the shallot.
Finish by whisking in Dijon mustard.
Whisk in a teaspoon or two of Asian fish sauce.
Add minced anchovy.
Swirl in more butter.

To Make a Quick Stock

There's a second option for those who would like to make a stock-based sauce without going to the trouble of creating a traditional stock or resorting to store-bought stock. While you're cooking your main dish, **SET** another sauté pan over medium-high heat and **SWEAT** some onion, carrot, and any bits of meat or cartilage that may have been trimmed from the main item. When they've become tender, a few minutes, **ADD** a cup of hot water and **DEGLAZE** the pan. **BOIL** on high till the water is gone and the vegetables begin to brown. Once the pan is dry and the vegetables are coloring, **ADD** another cup of hot water and **DO** the same. When the water has again cooked off, **ADD** a final cup of hot water and **BOIL** till it's reduced by a third. **SET** this aside until you're ready to make your pan sauce. **STRAIN** it into your pan sauce, pressing as much liquid out of the vegetables as you can.

Rémoulade

This is a centuries-old creation, a mayonnaise-based sauce that takes on different forms depending on the garnish—add Cajun spices and you're in Louisiana; if you're in the 1970s Midwest, it's tartar sauce and Mom's baking fish sticks in the oven; season it with cornichons and tarragon (as below) and you're transported to southern France. Feel free to spice up your rémoulade however you wish. It's a great all-purpose sauce for seafood, especially fried; I also like it on French fries or on a roast beef sandwich. In this book, I pair it with chicken schnitzel (page 53) and, spiked with sriracha, soft-shell crab sandwiches (page 103).

Rémoulade is best if you make your own mayonnaise, but feel free to use store-bought mayonnaise.

FOR THE MAYONNAISE:

1 egg yolk

2 teaspoons water

1 teaspoon fresh lemon juice

½ teaspoon salt

½ to ¾ cup/120 to 180 milliliters vegetable oil

MAKES ABOUT ½ TO ¾ CUP/150 TO 200 GRAMS MAYONNAISE

1 tablespoon fresh lemon juice

1 tablespoon minced shallot

1 tablespoon minced cornichons

1 tablespoon chopped capers

1 tablespoon chopped fresh tarragon

1 tablespoon sliced fresh chives

½ teaspoon Asian fish sauce

1 pinch or up to ⅛ teaspoon cayenne pepper

½ to ¾ cup/150 to 200 grams mayonnaise

MAKES ABOUT 1 CUP/240 MILLILITERS

TO MAKE THE MAYONNAISE:

- If you're making your own mayonnaise, **WHISK** to combine the yolk, water, lemon juice, and salt in a large mixing bowl. **ADD** a single drop of the oil to the bowl while still whisking vigorously. Then **BEGIN** to add the remaining oil in a thin, steady stream, whisking continuously, until all the oil is incorporated and you have a thick sauce that will hold a peak. Alternatively, you can **FOLLOW** the same procedure using a handheld blender with a whisk attachment.

TO MAKE THE RÉMOULADE:

- **COMBINE** the lemon juice and shallot and set aside for 10 minutes or longer.
- **STIR** the shallot mixture and all the remaining ingredients into the mayonnaise.

Cumberland Sauce

There were many German chefs in culinary school, and they liked to pair game with this sauce. Its predominant characteristic is the sweet-sour nature of currant, which perfectly complements any rich meat. I scarcely heard the name uttered outside of culinary school, though, and was glad to find that the estimable hunter-gatherer-cook Hank Shaw had written about it. I took Shaw's advice and paired it with venison (page 139), but it would be perfect with the sautéed duck on page 69, too. Currant jelly is fine to use, though I prefer a jammy confection (see the box on page 155) for its chunky nature and the way it helps thicken the sauce.

2 teaspoons vegetable oil (optional)

1 tablespoon minced shallot

2 teaspoons whole mustard seeds

**½ cup/120 milliliters full-bodied wine
(such as a decent Cabernet Sauvignon or zinfandel)**

½ cup/120 milliliters veal stock (or beef or chicken stock)

Kosher salt

¼ cup/45 grams currant jelly or jam

Zest of ½ an orange, plus juice squeezed from ¼ of the orange

Zest and juice from ½ a lemon

Cayenne pepper

MAKES ABOUT 1 CUP/240 MILLILITERS

- In the pan you used for sautéing (or in a clean pan in which you've heated the vegetable oil), **COOK** the shallot and mustard seeds over medium heat until the seeds begin to pop. **ADD** the wine and boil, scraping clean the bottom of the pan as you cook off most of the wine. When the wine is reduced to below the level of the mustard seeds, **ADD** the stock and **SEASON** the sauce with a four-finger pinch of salt. **REDUCE** the sauce by half. **ADD** the jelly or jam, orange juice, and lemon juice. **SIMMER** to combine all the flavors, then **ADD** the zests and a pinch or two of cayenne. **TASTE** for seasoning and **ADJUST** as necessary. **KEEP** warm until ready to serve.

To Make Currant Jam

If you have access to fresh currants, making your own jam is a must, as it is incomparable: a unique sweet-and-sour condiment for toast, popovers, or this sauce. **COMBINE** currants and half their weight in sugar (I used a quart container of currants, about 10 ounces/300 grams, with 5 ounces/150 grams sugar). **ADD** $\frac{1}{2}$ cup/120 milliliters water to dissolve the sugar, and **COOK** over low heat till the mixture is viscous. (When cooled it should be stiff enough to hold its shape.) This same technique can be used for just about any berry and is an excellent way to make use of leftover berries that may otherwise go bad.

Step 1. Cumberland sauce *mise en place*: stock, zest and juice from lemon and orange, cayenne, mustard seeds, shallots, wine, and currant jam.

Step 2. The shallot is softened in the cooking pan, and mustard seeds are added.

Step 3. Mustard seeds are toasted with the shallot.

Step 4. The pan is deglazed with red wine and the wine reduced.

Step 5. Stock is added and reduced before whisking in the currant jelly or jam and citrus zest and juices.

Guacamole

With most common kitchen preparations, the simpler the better. As Elise Bauer writes on her blog, Simply Recipes, all you really need for guacamole is ripe avocados and salt. True. In my version, I add shallot, my favorite onion, macerated in the juice of a lime and salted. I also throw in some red chiles for color and a little spice. If you want it hotter, add up to ¼ teaspoon cayenne pepper.

We almost always think of guacamole as a dip when, in fact, it makes a fabulous condiment for pork chops and a great topping for a burger or sautéed chicken. When guacamole is used as a sauce, I like it to be more acidic than I would for a basic chip dip. The amount of juice in a lime varies, so always hold some back and add more to taste.

2 tablespoons minced shallot

Juice of 1 lime

½ teaspoon kosher salt

2 ripe avocados

**1 red chile (such as serrano),
seeded if desired and minced (optional)**

Cayenne pepper (optional)

SERVES 4

- **COMBINE** the shallot, most of the lime juice, and the salt in a small bowl and **ALLOW** it to sit for 10 minutes. **HALVE** the avocados, **REMOVE** the pits, and **SCOOP** the flesh into a bowl or large mortar. **ADD** three-quarters of the shallot and lime mixture. **MASH** with a fork (or pestle) until you've reached the desired consistency—chunky or smooth is up to you. **TASTE** and **ADD** more shallot and lime juice as necessary. **STIR** in any additional garnish or seasonings you wish, such as minced chile and cayenne. **SERVE** immediately.

Step 1. Guacamole can be as simple as avocado, shallot, lime juice, salt, and cayenne.

Step 2. Add the avocado to the mortar or bowl after the shallots have macerated in the lime juice for 10 minutes or more.

Step 3. The avocado is mashed with a spoon or fork, mixed with the shallot and lime juice, and finished with fresh, minced red chiles.

Béchamel

This all-purpose sauce starter, known as a "mother sauce" in classic French cooking, is perfectly suited to the home kitchen because it uses ingredients we usually have on hand: milk, onion, flour, butter. It can be highly refined through cooking and straining, or it can be rustic, which is how I make it at home, without straining the shallots out of the sauce. Turn it into a sauce for an easy mac and cheese simply by adding any cheese that melts well, from cheddar to goat cheese to smoked Gouda. If you're in France, adding onion will turn it into a soubise sauce for Poulet Sauté Stanley (page 66); if you're in Oklahoma that same sauce will be called onion gravy and will be served with Chicken-Fried Steak (page 113). Add any additional flavors you wish—this milk-based sauce can be a powerful tool in your repertoire. (For a different mother sauce, chicken velouté, replace the milk with chicken stock and omit the nutmeg.)

2 tablespoons/30 grams butter

2 tablespoons minced shallot

Kosher salt

2 tablespoons flour

1½ cups/360 milliliters whole milk

Freshly grated nutmeg

MAKES ABOUT 1¼ CUPS/300 MILLILITERS

- **MELT** the butter in a small saucepan over medium heat. **ADD** the shallot and a four-finger pinch of salt and **COOK** till the shallot is soft and translucent, a couple of minutes.

- **ADD** the flour and **STIR** it around to cook it, another minute or so.

- **WHISK** in the milk and **CONTINUE** stirring, dragging a spatula or flat-edged wooden spoon across the bottom to keep the flour from sticking there. The milk will thicken as it heats. **ADD** a few gratings of nutmeg.

- The béchamel is ready to use as soon as it's thick, though it will improve if you **TURN** the heat to low, **PULL** the pan to the side of the burner, and **LET** it continue to cook, skimming the residue that collects at the cool side of the pan.

- **USE** immediately or **REFRIGERATE** in a covered container for up to 5 days. **REHEAT** gently over low heat; if on reheating the sauce is too thick, **THIN** it as desired with more milk.

Step 1. Béchamel *mise en place.*

Step 2. The shallot is first cooked in plenty of butter.

Step 3. The shallot should be cooked till tender but not browned.

Step 4. Flour is added to create a roux.

Step 5. Once the flour has been incorporated into the butter, milk is added.

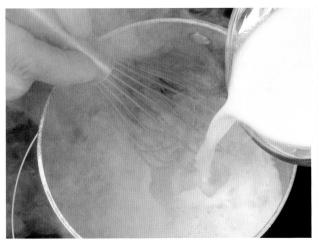

Step 6. Whisk to incorporate the milk into the roux.

Step 7. Stir, dragging a flat-edged wooden spatula along the bottom to ensure that the flour doesn't stick and scorch.

Step 8. The sauce should be thick once it begins to simmer, but cooking it gently enhances the flavor.

Step 9. Finish with gratings of nutmeg to taste.

Tarragon Butter (Compound Butter)

Compound butter makes for a quick sauce that can flavor anything from steak or hamburgers to roast chicken or fish. This version features tarragon, which I like to pair with flatiron steak (page 123), but you can use any soft herb that you have on hand, such as chives or parsley. Or use the same amount of cilantro and minced chipotle peppers in adobo sauce—this is especially good on grilled beef. I encourage you to improvise. Compound butter will keep for up to 2 weeks in the fridge or several months in the freezer.

1 teaspoon minced shallot

**1 teaspoon fresh lemon juice,
plus the minced zest from ¼ of the lemon**

Kosher salt

½ cup/120 grams butter, at room temperature

2 tablespoons minced fresh tarragon

2 teaspoons minced fresh parsley (optional)

MAKES ABOUT ½ CUP/115 GRAMS

- **COMBINE** the shallot and lemon juice in a small bowl and **STIR** so that all of the shallot comes in contact with the lemon juice. **ADD** a pinch of salt. **LET** sit for 10 minutes.

- In a mixing bowl, **COMBINE** the shallot and lemon mixture with the butter, zest, and herbs. **MIX** with a rubber spatula until all the ingredients are dispersed throughout the butter.

- The butter is ready to use or can be refrigerated for up to 5 days. For a neat appearance, **TRANSFER** the butter to a sheet of plastic. **FORM** it into a tight roll, twisting both ends and tying them off. **SUBMERGE** the roll in ice water till the butter has set to make a perfect cylinder. **REFRIGERATE** until ready to use, then **SLICE** into individual portions to serve.

Step 1. Compound butter *mise en place*: soft butter, tarragon and parsley, shallot macerated in lemon juice, and lemon zest.

Step 2. Combine all the ingredients in a bowl.

Step 3. Stir with a rubber spatula until the ingredients are uniformly incorporated.

Step 4. The butter is ready to use as is at this point.

Step 5. For an elegant appearance, transfer the butter to a sheet of plastic wrap.

Step 6. Roll the butter into a tight cylinder.

Step 7. Tie the ends of plastic wrap together and submerge in an ice bath until the butter is fully chilled.

Step 8. Slice into discs to serve atop hot beef, chicken, or fish.

Tzatziki

I always pair this sauce with lamb meatballs (page 133) and lamb burgers (page 137), but it's also a great all-purpose dipping sauce for pita, chips, or vegetables. If you increase the amount of cucumber and add 1 teaspoon ground cumin and ¼ teaspoon cayenne pepper, you have the Indian salad raita.

1 tablespoon minced shallot

1 teaspoon minced garlic

1 to 2 tablespoons fresh lemon juice

Kosher salt

½ cup/75 grams peeled and small-diced English cucumber

1 cup/225 grams plain Greek-style yogurt

¼ cup/5 grams minced fresh mint

½ teaspoon freshly ground black pepper

MAKES ABOUT 1½ CUPS/325 GRAMS

- In a small bowl, **COMBINE** the shallot and garlic with 1 tablespoon of the lemon juice and **GIVE** it a three-finger pinch of salt. **SET** aside to macerate for 10 minutes.

- **COMBINE** the cucumber, yogurt, mint, and pepper. **SPOON** the shallot and garlic into the mix. **ADD** another aggressive pinch of salt, **STIR**, and **TASTE**. **ADD** more lemon juice as needed. The mixture should be very lemony and minty.

EQUIPMENT &
TOOLS

THE STOVETOP

Gas burners remain my preferred heat source. Many professional kitchens and some homes have graduated flat tops, heavy iron surfaces that are very hot at the center, with decreasing heat as you move farther from the center. A relatively new entry into the kitchen is the induction burner, which heats steel and iron with electromagnetic currents. It's a very efficient form of cooking with many advantages—almost all the cooking shots in this book were done on an induction cooktop. The only disadvantage is that it works only if your pan is iron or steel, not aluminum or glass. The least desirable heat source is an electric burner, because it's slow to heat and slow to cool, which makes it difficult to control the heat of your pan. If this is what you have, I recommend you allow the coil to heat before putting the pan on it and, of course, remove the pan from the coil when you've finished cooking the food, rather than simply turning the burner off.

THE COOKING VESSEL

Every kitchen should have two high-quality, stainless-steel sauté pans, small (8 inches/20 centimeters) and large (12 inches/30 centimeters). They should be heavy for uniform heating and have a metal handle so that you can use them in a hot oven. A good nonstick pan for specific items can come in handy; just don't make this your default sauté pan. For most sautés, stainless steel is best, but I also recommend cast-iron skillets, preferably the older ones that don't have a coating on the metal, as most of the contemporary pans seem to have. (See pages 2 to 3 for more on pans.)

THE SPATULA

Metal or plastic spatulas are essential tools for flipping food you're sautéing. My favorite kind of spatula is called a fish spatula. It's triangular and slightly offset, with a thin blade for slipping under the food, and it's slotted so that it doesn't lift oil or sauce along with what you're flipping. Some chefs prefer a palette knife, a long, blunt flat blade typically used for icing cakes. The one turning device you should be careful with is a pair of tongs. Tongs can easily damage what you're cooking, so use them thoughtfully. For instance, you would always want to flip a fish fillet with a spatula, not tongs.

SIDE TOWELS

This item is among the most important tools in my kitchen, something used daily for grabbing hot pans. Side towels offer much more control than pot holders and oven mitts, which are a hindrance (and look silly besides). Buy a few good side towels (such as the ones from JB Prince) and keep them at the ready for sauté-pan handles that have become hot or for retrieving sauté pans from a hot oven.

THE MEAT MALLET

I have one and love it for tenderizing meats and flattening pieces of meat that have uneven thicknesses. It's nice to have, but a small, heavy skillet can do much of the same work.

THE SAUTÉ
LARDER

• SALT

Kosher salt should be your default salt. If you always use the same brand, you can learn to gauge salt by touch. Fine sea salt and finishing salt, such as the delicately crunchy Maldon (my favorite), are great to have on hand to add color, texture, and flavor to soft foods.

• FAT

Inexpensive vegetable oil is the most useful fat for sautéing anything over high heat. An inexpensive but flavorful olive oil is also a good sautéing fat for those foods that don't require high heat; I particularly like to sauté vegetables in olive oil. Butter can be a good, low-temperature fat to use for sauté; remember, though, that it will stay cool until the water cooks out of it, and then the solids can burn. For this reason, clarified butter (from which the solids have been removed—see page 4) is a better option. Butter is also a great fat with which to finish sautéed food, whether in a com-pound butter (page 164) or in a pan sauce (pages 148 to 151).

• DAIRY

In addition to butter, a well-stocked kitchen always has some half-and-half on hand. Half-and-half, like butter, is one step away from a finished sauce. It can be added to most of the dishes in this collection for a creamy finish. Of course, you can instead use cream if you want the finished sauce or soup to be very rich, but I find cream to be too heavy if used as the main sauce base; I prefer to use a small amount of cream to finish a dish if necessary, as one would mount butter into a sauce. When you use milk in cooking, as for the béchamel (page 160), choose whole milk; it is the most nutritious and delicious.

• WINE

Both white and red wine are flavorful liquids that can be added to the pan to deglaze it, lift the flavorful, browned protein off the pan, and become part of the finished sauce.

• SHALLOT

If you've spent any time with my recipes, you've surely run into plenty of minced shallot. Shallot is one of those magical elements that so easily elevate any number of sauces, whether a mayonnaise, vinaigrette, or simple pan sauce. Shallots need to be either cooked or, if used raw, macerated in an acidic liquid (vinegar or citrus juice) to soften their harsher nature. My kitchen is hobbled when I am out of shallots.

• FRESH HERBS

I finish many sauté dishes with minced soft herbs—usually parsley, tarragon, chervil (which is tarragon-like), chives, or cilantro. Thyme, which is considered a hard herb because of its hard stem, can also be used—simply pick the leaves from the stem.

• DRIED SPICES

Spices add great flavor to sautés and are typically used early in the cooking, added to the hot pan to cook slightly before the main item is cooked. The spices I rely on most are black pepper, cayenne pepper, coriander, and cumin.

• LEMON

You should always have a lemon or two on hand. The zest and juice are almost as powerful as salt in terms of their ability to enhance and finish most sautéed food.

• WHITE WINE VINEGAR

Like lemon, a high-quality white wine vinegar can elevate the sauce for many sautéed dishes, and is of course the go-to choice for most vinaigrettes. A selection of good vinegars gives you more options, but white wine vinegar is the most versatile.

• STOCK

I can't emphasize enough the difference that homemade stock makes in home cooking. Every store-bought broth I've found has some kind of added "natural flavor" or other ingredient you wouldn't use at home. These *un*natural flavors, when used to make a reduction sauce, become concentrated and overpowering. As for low-sodium broths, why do they need any sodium at all? The answer is to make up for a lack of authentic flavor. Stock making need not be a laborious affair. Make small quantities using leftover bones, carrot, and onion. Freeze what you won't use in the course of a week. When you have good stock, a fabulous sauce is moments away (see page 150).

ACKNOWLEDGMENTS

FIRST, THANKS GO TO DONNA, WHO PHOTOGRAPHED ALL the recipes in this book. Without her partnership, I could not have created these books.

Michael Sand, the book's editor at Little, Brown, helped create this series of technique books, and his editorial guidance has been invaluable. Michael Szczerban stepped into Michael Sand's shoes to help me finish the job. My copyeditor, Karen Wise, caught hundreds of errors and inconsistencies, proving that books are a team effort. Included in this team are other invaluable members of Little, Brown: Jayne Yaffe Kemp, Cathy Gruhn, Meghan Deans, Garrett McGrath, and Olivia Aylmer.

Enormous thanks, as always, go to my recipe testers, Marlene Newell, who not only tests the recipes but also keeps us all organized, and Matthew Kayahara.

Emilia Juocys, my assistant, not only keeps track of my working life but also serves as a kind of personal trainer of the spirit when motivation and energy flag.

INDEX

Page numbers in *italics* refer to photographs.

ABOUT THE AUTHOR

Michael Ruhlman is the bestselling and James Beard Award–winning author of many classic culinary books, including *The Making of a Chef, Egg, Ratio, The Elements of Cooking*, and *Charcuterie*. He lives in Cleveland, Ohio.